James Woodward is an Anglican Priest working in a unique Foundation which consists of a Parish Church, a Centre for the care of older people and a Church School. He is the Director of the Leveson Centre for the Study of Ageing, Spirituality and Social Policy and has written widely in the area of pastoral and practical theology. For further information about his work, visit <www.leveson.org.uk>. The author can be contacted via the web page.

Befriending Death

James Woodward

First published in Great Britain in 2005 by
Society for Promoting Christian Knowledge
36 Causton Street
London SW1P 4ST
www.spckpublishing.co.uk

The author and publisher have made every effort to ensure that the
external website and email addresses included in this book are correct and
up to date at the time of going to press. The author and publisher are not
responsible for the content, quality or continuing accessibility of the sites.

The publisher and author acknowledge with thanks permission to
reproduce extracts from the following:
Macmillan for 'The Kingdom' from *H'm*, a collection of poems by
R. S. Thomas, 1972.
Bloodaxe Books for *Anne Stevenson, The Collected Poems: 1955–1985*.

*Every effort has been made to acknowledge fully the sources of
material reproduced in this book. The publisher apologizes for any
omissions that may remain and, if notified, will ensure that full
acknowledgements are made in a subsequent edition.*

Scripture quotations are from the New Revised Standard Version of the
Bible, copyright © 1989 by the Division of Christian Education of the
National Council of the Churches of Christ in the USA.
Used by permission. All rights reserved.

British Library Cataloguing-in-Publication Data
A catalogue record for this book is available from the British Library

ISBN 978–0–281–05370–4

Designed and typeset by Kenneth Burnley, Wirral, Cheshire
First printed in Great Britain by Bookmarque
Subsequent digital printing in Great Britain

Produced on paper from sustainable forests

Contents

For my friends in the community of St Mary's,
Temple Balsall, with gratitude

Preface

This short book is addressed to the Christian reader who wants to have the opportunity to reflect not only on the place and meaning of death in life but also on the issues that loss or change confront us with. The book offers the reader the opportunity to reflect, feel and explore. It encourages a dialogue between the resources of the Christian tradition and our life experience.

The book is designed to be used alone or with others. A number of exercises and questions for reflection are contained within each chapter to facilitate the reader's further considerations and engagement with death. It also offers resources for those who may need some practical help or wish to learn more about topics or areas of discussion. The book is written for those who want to embrace the realities of death and those who stand in the presence of death.

The reader should realize that this book requires a certain amount of mental agility. It will become apparent that some parts are addressed particularly to those who care for the very sick and the dying, others to those close to death themselves, others to a more general audience. This moving of the searchlight is deliberate. All of us, at different times, may come into any or all of these categories. The hope is that readers will use their imaginations as the focus changes and make the necessary act of sympathy.

Readers may also notice a glaring omission: this book does not deal with the subject of life after death. This too is deliberate. The subject is so many-sided that adequate treatment would make this a very different book. The life that prepares for death is our subject.

This book is not and never could be the last word on death because the author is still growing and dying, living and changing, still open in mind and heart, and sometimes perplexed by the whole experience. It is a discourse of discovery; a meeting and connecting that is open-ended. The aim of the book is to invite us all into a deeper engagement. The challenge for us all is to integrate the experience of dying so that it can be part of our living and loving.

Acknowledgements

The journey of this book started for me nearly 20 years ago when I had the privilege of working at St Christopher's Hospice in south London prior to training for ministry. The reflections from that time have been shaped, challenged and affirmed by many since then. I would like to thank all those who in my ministry have enriched the growing: Consett Parish Church; the Bishop and Diocese of Oxford; the Queen Elizabeth Hospital, Birmingham; the parishes of Middleton and Wishaw; the CARA community in London; and finally the community of the Foundation of Lady Katherine Leveson in Temple Balsall.

I am grateful to the following who offered helpful comments on earlier drafts of the text: Leslie Houlden, Mark Pryce and Jenny Jones. Liz Marsh and Ruth McCurry at SPCK have been the most patient and encouraging of editors.

Christ Crucified, by Nigel Dwyer (see back cover) reproduced by courtesy of the artist.

1

Exploring the Theme – Dying to Live

Put a limit on time and every day counts.

Be patient towards all that is unresolved in your heart. Do not now seek the answers that cannot be given you because you would not be able to live them out. But love the questions and live everything. LIVE the questions now. Perhaps you will then gradually, without noticing it, live into the answer some distant day.

It would be surprising if many of us had spent much time and energy looking death in the face. Most of us desire a life of peace and contentment where our anxieties are contained and some of the harsher or more fearful aspects of life are kept under control or just faced when they occur.

Some have little alternative but to face the reality of loss and death. The unexpected diagnosis of cancer; the loss of parents; adapting to life without dependent children; coping with transitions and older age – these and other life experiences confront us with a number of questions and challenges which we face in all kinds of different ways.

Our past experiences and memories shape us too. All aspects of our past combine to make us the kind of people we are today: for good and ill. We all have to live with the choices we have made and the experiences that shape our lives. The key theme of this book is that the way that we embrace our dying within our living is fundamental to our well-being, our hopes, our fears, our loves and our salvation.

The theme of *living our dying* is based on three convictions. The first is that death in itself is not important. It is not charged with meaning, though for those left it is often fraught with meaning; death is simply the point or moment when a person ceases to live. What then is important is not death but dying. Our time of dying *can* be a futile struggling against dying and a fight to go on living. This is why embracing or befriending our dying is so significant.

The second conviction is that what we call living can in fact be rightly seen as dying. We are all dying and embracing a range of losses throughout our lives. We are all living in a dying situation, diminishing constantly and reacting to the experiences that make for our diminishment. It is worth looking back at some of the key points of our biographies and asking how these events or experiences have shaped the meaning and depth of the course of our lives. (See the Stepping stones exercise, p. 5.)

The third conviction is that our struggle to live in the light of coming death is always charged with meaning. In part our salvation depends upon what sense we make of it all in the light of our faith in God. This is why this subject is such an opportunity and challenge – worthy of all the attention paid to it by writers, poets, preachers and artists.

This also explains the urgency and necessity for us to address this area of our existence. We are involved now in the contradictions between life and death before death takes place, a tension which is partly a surrender to dying and partly a fight against dying. Our lives are a wonderful and mysterious mixture of giving up and not giving up, of surrender and resistance. In these paradoxes, in both aspects, both living our dying and dying to live, we encounter God.

One of my earliest childhood memories of death centres on the death of my great-grandmother in a small mining village in the north-east of England. I was about five years of age. I remember my blind great-gran playing with me on her knee and felt the mystery of why she could see so much with her eyes closed. I couldn't understand why she was absent one day and why members of the family were crying. When she died, the family kept vigil and the only role for the undertaker was to leave the coffin at the house. The family did the rest and the body lay under the window in the front room. It was into this gathering that I moved freely and was lifted up by a relative to see her in the coffin. I touched her cold face and said goodbye.

Modern death is very different. Perhaps we are as a result impoverished. We push it away and distance ourselves from it. There seems to be little chance for much intimacy in our mourning. The cold space of the modern crematorium allows us to see but not touch – somehow to distance ourselves from the realities of dying. But in fact we are dying all the time and we must ask ourselves what we do with this reality.

As soon as we are born we begin to die. We all live and grow but before us is the reality of the end of life. Our lives are an amazing mixture of living and dying – a continual series of dyings, and deaths leading to new life, which make up the pattern of human existence, the Passover pattern of growth into new life by way of diminishment and death.

Our lives are made up of a complex series of losses,

changes, movements, partings and endings. The child in us has to die before we become an independent teenager, and we do not become such until we have put away some of the cosy privileges and protectedness of the child. There is also a parallel transition going on in the life of parents who have to put away the protective attitudes appropriate to the parents of a child and learn the new, more risky and trusting attitudes appropriate to the parents of adolescents.

Another area of life where we successively die to be reborn is that of parting. I never get used to parting either from people or places. The places where I have lived and worked twine themselves around my heart like ivy round a tree trunk. Every corner has a memory that can tug at the heart. Leaving people is, of course, even more difficult than leaving places.

Yet we know that unless we part from one place and stage in life we cannot begin in another. Sometimes our affection for the old has to be released and purified before we can treat the new with seriousness and respect. So it is with colleagues and friends. However heart-rending the break-up of a partnership, it often has to happen quite brutally in order that we can grow and work seriously with other partners or associates. To refuse to accept the death of one relationship can hamper the making of new ones. Here is an example where growth begins with a walking away and a letting go. Indeed the love is often proved in the letting go.

Sometimes the parting is not of our choosing or indeed negotiated by us, and that can be painful. Others may make the decisions that shape our lives and losses. It is very hard in these circumstances not to feel a kind of death and rejection. Failing to get a job, compulsory redundancy, bereavement, sudden death and failed love are all examples of the experiences of dying and loss that make up our lives.

The chapters that follow invite you into a deeper engagement with the realities of death and dying in your life experiences in order to deepen, enrich and widen sympathy and feeling for living hopefully.

Stepping stones

The aims of this exercise are to look at our life as a whole; to explore its movement and continuity from a new perspective. When we speak of stepping stones we mean the events that come into our minds when we reflect on the course that our life has taken from birth to the present moment. Stepping stones are the significant points of movement along the road of our life.

1   Take a plain piece of paper and mark across it ten circles that would act like stepping stones across a river.
2   Relax. Place yourself in the presence of God. Be still and know God's love. Allow your breathing to become lower, softer and more relaxed.
3   Think of your life as a whole. Feel the movement of your living as a flowing and continuous movement like a river through many changes and phases.
4   Places, images, people, words, events may come into your mind. Your place of birth, your first school, a holiday, an experience of love . . . Hang on to these images. Think of a descriptive phrase that sums up each of them. I loved . . . I got lost . . . Write it down. Avoid self-judgement or analysis.
5   Label on the paper the ten stepping stones of your life.

Each stepping stone will represent a thread of continuity, or lasting feature about your life stage at the present moment. Each has helped to form the 'you' of the present. Some of the stepping stones will be factual, drawn from the vital events of your life (for example, a career step); some may be qualitative events (for example, getting married or coming to faith) that will carry the maturity and private meaning in your life.

These stepping stones can be constructed from different vantage points.

For example, you could try to see them in the context of your journey of faith or of the way your attitudes to other people have developed.

Are these stages and experiences marked by 'dying' as well as living?

Questions for further reflection

- What are your earliest experiences of death?
- What has helped you to cope with life transitions, losses and changes?
- Do you give time to reflecting on your dying?

Life and death

The aim of this exercise is to explore what we feel makes for life in our faith.

Take a piece of paper and divide it into two columns. Head one side *Events that bring me to life* and the other *Events that deaden me*. Then read the passage below and compile your list.

Before the world was made we were chosen to live in God's presence by praising, reverencing and serving him in and through his creation.

As one, because God alone is our security, refuge and strength.

We can be so detached from every created thing only if we have a stronger attachment; therefore our one dominating desire and fundamental choice must be to live in love in his presence. Everything on the face of the earth exists to help us to do this; we must appreciate and make use of everything that helps, and rid ourselves of anything that is destructive to our living in love in his presence.

Therefore, we must be so poised that we do not cling to any created thing as though it were our ultimate good, but remain open to the possibility that love may demand of us poverty rather than riches, sickness rather than health, dishonour rather than honour, a short life rather than a long one.

Does this give you any indication of the events or experiences that are destructive or creative of life in you?

Questions for further reflection

- What losses in life have been most significant for you?
- Who or what has helped you cope with them?
- Have you ever been able to thank God for a loss, knowing that some kind of gain has been achieved?

2

Spirituality and Dying

It's a long way off but inside it
There are quite different things going on:
Festivals at which the poor man
Is king and the consumptive is
Healed; mirrors in which the blind look
At themselves and love looks at them
Back; and industry is for mending
The bent bones and the minds fractured
By life. It's a long way off, but to get
There takes no time and admission
Is free, if you will purge yourself
Of desire, and present yourself with
Your need only and the simple offering
Of your faith, green as a leaf.
(R. S. Thomas)

O LORD, *you know; remember me and visit me.*
(Jeremiah 15.15)

Joy and Woe are woven fine
A clothing for the soul divine
Under every grief and pine
Lies a joy with silken twine

It is right it should be so
Man was made for joy and woe
And when this we rightly know
Through the world we safely go.
(William Blake)

Our treasure lies in our inner life. It is our inner life that affects our perceptions of the world and determines our actions in it and reactions to it. We often tend to ignore our inner life but it refuses to be ignored and finds expression in all kinds of ways. Sometimes our inner life can erupt as we find ourselves caught up in emotions and feelings that are hard to control or run away from. Think, for example, of the frustration of a tired parent who hits their child in anger, or the profound sense of loneliness that can overcome us when we are at our busiest.

In religious language, this inner life is the soul. The religious adventure is the art of knowing it, healing it and harmonizing its forces. The art of befriending our destiny and ourselves is part of the journey of exploring our spirituality and discovering how this spirituality can be woven into the fabric of our loving and growing. Religion should help us to trust our own feelings and to become more aware of our inner feelings as the signs and pointers towards meaning, purpose and depth. This inner life needs to be trusted as a source of both strength and wisdom.

Listening to other voices

The following three stories come from my own pastoral experience and they give us a number of clues about how we might embrace and befriend our destiny.

Margaret is a doctor who had just given birth to a baby boy. I bumped into her outside the hospital chapel and within minutes she spilled out her story. She felt paralysed by the grief of the loss of her mother some months before. In this grief she questioned her responsibility for her mother's death. Now she was able neither to face the loss of her mother nor to celebrate fully the birth of her baby and welcome him into life. These two coinciding experiences, birth and death, had left her numb and suspended. We talked, and gradually connections were made as thoughts and feelings were expressed. Margaret expressed her emotions and came to let go of her mother and celebrate her son's birth. Slowly hope and joy found a way back into her life.

Imagine a busy hospital on Christmas Eve. A group of people from local churches gather for carol singing around the wards. Carefully and simply, the well-known words are sung. Many are uplifted and comforted by this experience. For others the celebration of Jesus' birth is a reminder of the fragility of their humanity and it brings them to tears. To listen to the celebration of life comforts, changes and reassures, but it also saddens as it recalls truth about ourselves.

My third voice is most vividly before me as an inspiration and example. Elizabeth knew that her healing could not mean cure and she faced her cancer and her dying with honesty and courage. She talked and raged and laughed and cried about her life, and when death came she was prepared. In one of those unique moments after we said the Lord's Prayer together I commended her living and dying to God with the words, 'Elizabeth, go forth upon your journey from this world.' She died. Her family sat with her and shared their memories, their hopes and

11

fears. There was relief that her suffering was no more and joy that she had lived so fully and given so much.

The common threads in all of these stories are easy to identify: coming clean and facing facts honestly; encountering suffering, pain and loss; drawing close to people and refusing to be isolated; asking for and accepting help; confronting the reality and finality of death and being able and willing to be vulnerable.

One thread relates very much to our theme and it is easy to overlook in our death-denying society. We are perhaps conditioned to avoid confronting fear, to avoid the wilderness and the desert places in our own hearts and world. We live under a kind of tyranny of certainty where strength, confidence, life, success and security dominate our emotional, social, ecclesiastical and political lives. In our healing we seek those things that reassure us rather than those things that speak of our fears and doubts. We do not like to give way to these feelings. This is hardly surprising – it takes courage to stay with our doubts, pains and insecurities.

Margaret and Elizabeth ask us to think about where our strength and security lie. They ask us to think about how *meaning* (and not mere 'happening') is part of our lives. From what base do we start? Frightened individuals build frightened societies. Fearful Christians build fearful lives where uncertainty, contradiction, paradox and ambiguity are dealt with by going for false security, strength and certainty. Instead of drawing people together, fear polarizes: it separates and isolates people, issues, organizations, communities and nations. Margaret and Elizabeth ask us, through their lives, to face our own and each other's vulnerability and dying. For when we are vulnerable, we are stripped of affectation and self-deceit.

12

There can be healing and growth when we accept our need of others, when we let go of our independence and our drives to succeed and give. To give is to be powerful; to receive is to be vulnerable. The gospel, in this and other contexts, demands that we are drawn out of the tyranny of certainty and that we hold together the paradoxes and contradictions between life and death, faith and fear, hope and despair, love and hate, alienation and relationship, fragmentation and connectedness.

The voices from the hospital on Christmas Eve are of particular significance here. Why were some patients so comforted by the singing of those carols? The boy child, hymned so crisply, so purely, is a sacrifice. Of course not all carols mention explicitly his death; but the birth of Christ is part of the same offering, the same sacrifice, which is completed on the cross. It is for his self-offering that Christmas exalts God's gift in this lowly baby.

Perhaps we sometimes too easily become accustomed to the starkness of the imagery and the meaning of Christian symbolism. Too often religion opts for purity, clarity and distance. We need to explore how the necessary Christian connections are made for us. Our discipleship, in its following of Christ, affirms a trust in the death of Christ and its power to create new life, to transform all of our living and dying.

Perhaps the gospel message offers us only a certain promise of uncertainty, of continuing loss and change. It reminds us that comprehending mystery is the process of discovering and engaging with the struggle to manage these profound ambiguities and paradoxes as a condition of our living. It is about being in touch with our weaknesses and vulnerabilities as the bases of our living, loving and dying.

To affirm this as our spiritual base is not to give up hope – but to bring all of what we are into the truth and reality of God. It is to encourage both each other and ourselves into a more trusting and passionate response to the death of Christ as it connects with our own dying. For in this act we are given the sign of the love of God. The way of Christ – our co-traveller – is a road by which we can come home to ourselves and to one another. Our solutions need to be grounded, honest and human solutions leading to the peace and justice for which we long.

That is why listening to the voices of those who embrace their experiences of dying is so important and why Margaret and Elizabeth have so much to teach us. They show us that to live we too must die. To love is to risk the pain of loss. It is a modern lie that there can be love without pain and without sacrifice, and that our desire is completed in the love of pleasure only. Such passion is fantasy and will pass away. True love is a love that suffers – the love of God, which is the passion of Christ – a suffering love, which millions have found to be the source of life. Here is a death worth living for.

Practical considerations

The issues raised in this chapter are not simply abstract and theoretical; they have practical implications for us all. These include:

- We are all going to die! We cannot go through life pretending that we will live for ever. To consider our death is not to have a morbid fascination with it but to recognize the inevitability of it. The more time we give to consider death the better we shall be able to face loss and change. The more we consider death calmly and in good time then the more creatively we shall be able to deal with it when it has to be faced. We can make a friend of death.

- While it might be comforting to think that there is no need to prepare for dying and that we may well die in our sleep, this is not the usual pattern of death. For most of us there will be at least a little forewarning of death, and hence a period of time when we have to confront this knowing as best we can.
- It is also unrealistic to assume that caring for the dying can be left to hospitals or doctors. Many people will die at home, and even those in hospitals will have friends and family as part of the process of dying.

Your own obituary notice

This may seem an odd and morbid suggestion!

Imagine that you have had a long life. Then write the obituary, which in your wildest dreams you would love to have. Do not analyse it or think about it in too much detail – allow your imagination to run free. Give rein to your ambition and hopes as well as the factual realities.

- How closely in touch with your inner life do you feel?
- What does your piece of writing say about your own desires?
- How would you like to determine the direction of your life in the light of this obituary?

3

For Those Who Listen

Listen

*When I ask you to listen to me and you start giving
    me advice,*
you have not done what I asked.

When I ask you to listen to me
and you begin to tell me why I shouldn't feel that way
you are trampling on my feelings.

When I ask you to listen to me
*and you feel you have to do something to solve my
    problems*
you have failed me, strange as that may seem.

LISTEN! All I asked was that you listen
Not talk or do – just hear me.
Advice is cheap; 25 cents will get you Dear Abby and
Billy Graham in the same newspaper,
And I can do it for myself; I'm not helpless,
Maybe discouraged and faltering, but not helpless.

*When you do something for me that I can and need
    to do*
for myself, you contribute to my fear and weakness.

*But when you accept as a single fact that I do feel
    what I feel,
no matter how irrational, then I quit trying to
    convince
you and can get about the business of understanding
what's behind this irrational feeling.
And when that's clear, the answers are obvious and I
don't need advice.
Irrational feelings make sense when we understand
    what's behind them.*

*Perhaps that's why prayer works, because God is
    often silent and He
doesn't give advice or try to 'fix' things. He listens and
    often silently helps you work it out.*

*So please listen and just hear me, and if you want to
    talk,
wait a minute for your turn and I'll listen to you.*

(Anonymous)

Seeing

There is an ancient Hindu fable about understanding something one cannot see. The fable goes something like this:

The Blind Men and the Elephant

There were once six blind men who stood by the roadside every day and begged from the people who passed. They had often heard of elephants, but they had never seen one; for, being blind, how could they?

18

It so happened one morning that an elephant was driven down the road where they stood. When they were told that the great beast was before them, they asked the driver to let them stop so they might see him.

Of course they could not see him with their eyes, but thought by touching him they could learn just what kind of animal he was.

The first one happened to put his hand on the elephant's side. 'Well, well,' he said, 'now I know all about the beast. He is exactly like a wall.'

The second felt the elephant's tusk. 'My brother,' he said, 'you are mistaken. He is not like a wall, he is round and smooth and sharp. He is more like a spear than anything else.'

The third happened to take hold of the elephant's trunk. 'Both of you are wrong,' he said. 'Anybody who knows anything can see that the elephant is like a snake.'

The fourth reached out his arms, and grasped one of the elephant's legs. 'Oh, how blind you are,' he said. 'It's very plain to me that he is round and tall like a tree.'

The fifth was a very tall man, and he chanced to take hold of the elephant's ear. 'The blindest man ought to know that this beast is not like any of these things that you name,' he said. 'He is exactly like a huge fan.'

The sixth was very blind indeed, and it took some time before he could find the elephant at all. At last he seized the animal's tail. 'Oh, foolish fellows!' he cried. 'You surely have lost your senses. This animal is not like a wall, or a spear, or a snake, or a tree; neither like a fan. But any man with a particle of sense can see that he is exactly like a rope.'

Then the elephant moved on, and the six blind men sat by the roadside all day, and quarrelled about him. Each believed that he knew just how the animal looked; and each called the others hard names because they did not agree with him. People who have eyes sometimes act as foolishly.

The Moral: People are likely to disagree vastly when they are concentrating on different parts of the same thing.

It is the purpose of this chapter to explore some of the issues that emerge out of the difficult experience of being told news about illness and death. It offers some pointers for consideration and practical implications to be reflected on for people who respond to those facing a terminal diagnosis.

We have acknowledged that we are not used to talking about death; and when we do it, it is often in very general terms. Rarely do we talk specifically about our own death, or that of the person to whom we are speaking. The consequence of this is that when we do have to talk about death we are often ill-prepared to do so. Advance thought can improve matters.

Breaking bad news

Experience teaches that often people believe that patients who are dying should not be told. Practically everyone seems disinclined to tell. However, when one asks people what they themselves would like to know, a very different picture emerges. The vast majority of people say that they would like to be told the whole truth of what is happening to them. The lesson seems to be that we underestimate the ability of others to cope. Perhaps the difficulty lies in our own reluctance to talk about death and dying.

How best should we think about this sensitive area? What principles might guide our action and responses?

1 *Adequate preparation*

When we are faced with difficult tasks, time spent in preparation is valuable. So that we can work out how news and information can best be shared with others, we need to consider carefully how to tell each of those who are going to be involved.

2 *Build up trust*

Where one whose death is drawing nearer is concerned, the more he or she is able to build up trust, the easier it is for them to accept what is said. Unless this is done, we cannot tell how people will react. Some may be so shocked that they are unable to absorb the information that is shared. Others will surprise us with their ability to cope – the news often gives them confirmation of what they already instinctively knew. It will be important to give the process time and sensitivity.

3 *Continuing communication*

An important aspect of breaking bad news is that the process of communication is a continuing task. People should expect to have their further questions answered and anxieties engaged with. There will also be an ongoing need for information after the news has been broken.

4 *Telling others*

The person may need help to think through whom they want to tell. They may want to reflect on how they should tell family, friends or work colleagues.

5 *General advice*

Dos and don'ts – for those who share the news and those receiving it:

- Do feel free to break the news in your own time.
- Do remember that listening can be as important as speaking.
- Do admit if you feel awkward or embarrassed – attempts to cover this up can be misinterpreted.
- Do allow the person you tell – or the person you hear – to respond to you.
- Do try to discover facts about treatment or prognosis that may help you to understand the person and their predicament.
- Do recognize that practical help may be as important as other kinds and may help the sufferer to be reconciled.
- Don't try to steer the conversation away from death; this doesn't necessarily provide comfort, and can give the impression that discussion isn't allowed.
- Don't feel awkward if the person shows signs of being upset or begins to cry; give them permission in word or manner to express their feelings in whatever way is appropriate and natural.
- Don't make offers of help unless you are sure that you can fulfil them.
- Don't pass on the news to anyone else unless this has been agreed.
- Don't demand any justification for a person's behaviour – for example, if on hearing they respond with, 'Why didn't you tell me before?'
- Don't start treating the person as helpless and as needing everything doing for them.

- Don't treat the person as now in a new, depersonalized zone.

Just as the reactions of the dying person will change and adapt, so will those of the people participating in the knowledge. It is possible that if time and care are spent in communication, then all can work together to provide mutual support.

For yourself

- If you are given the news that your own life may be limited, be prepared to take in the information one step at a time. Feel free to ask for further information as and when you require it.
- Tell someone close to you as soon as possible. If you need help to do this, then ask the person who told you. Try to decide who else should know and how and what they should be told. Be determined in passing on the news; don't be tempted to wait for the right time – there isn't one.
- Beware of the temptation not to tell people. While this may sometimes be appropriate, remember that they may well find out anyway, and perhaps be hurt by your lack of trust in them.
- Be prepared for a variety of responses from people and be careful not to read too much into them. Embarrassment and awkwardness are natural when venturing into unfamiliar territory.
- If you receive the news that a loved one is dying, be as honest and open as you can, about both your own feelings and those of others. Acknowledge that it will

be a difficult time for everyone and try to help each other to cope.

Listening to other voices

Mark

No amount of knowledge can really help you face being told that you are about to die. My emotions during this period of adaptation and reconciliation were so intense and enduring that I find it hard to share them with you. Someone once said to me, 'There is no way out of the desert except through it,' and this certainly reflects my own experience.

I felt befuddled, in a swamp, engulfed by the enormity of what surrounded me. It was hard to believe that I would survive these feelings, let alone endure the physical loss of my body.

At first it was hard to know who to believe, and part of me doubted that what the 'expert' was telling me was true. I felt shock, some denial and confusion. Then I just kept feeling angry, especially when I looked around and realized how much I was going to miss; my partner, the house and garden that I had worked so hard on, and the retirement that I had made careful plans for. Here was the real frustration. I didn't want to die and I was power-less to do anything.

Perhaps the biggest surprise was, after years of going to church, the spiritual emptiness that I experienced. I expected there to be more help and comfort from my faith. Instead it became a focus for my disillusionment and anger. Where was God in my hour of need?

Jane

I have been working over the past five years with people living with terminal disease. It emerged out of my own bereavement – after my partner's death I wanted to do something to help others.

One aspect of this work concerns communication. I have found that it is important to help others to accept the physical reality of their dying. Some people cope by pretending that it simply isn't happening. We need to work together to create a climate that encourages and supports open and honest conversation. All this needs to be taken at the pace of the person living with dying. We are all unique and we often communicate in different ways – and we must allow for that diversity.

It is important to be realistic and flexible – people don't change habits of expression and communication overnight and we all need the support and space to cope in our own way. Anxiety and depression are key emotions to be embraced and worked with. Above all, the individual needs to be enabled to make as many of their own decisions as possible.

A second key area is the question of an individual's spiritual concerns. Death raises fundamental questions about life. Why are we here? What does life mean? What is a good life? Have I achieved anything of value? I think that part of my own role, as a caregiver, is to help the individual in thinking about their answers to these questions.

Spiritual questions are not dealt with easily. For some people, faith gives answers and comfort. For others it is a cause of uncertainty and insecurity, perhaps because of the kind of religious teaching they have absorbed. Faith can cause difficulty for those who do not feel comforted by prayer or spiritual aids. I have found that it is important for these people to feel that their concerns and questions are a normal and reasonable part of the process. It is sometimes helpful to explore which beliefs are helpful and which are a cause for anxiety. I have had to learn to accept diversity of views and perspectives and to appreciate the range of things that support – or else distress – people in faith.

Practical considerations

The process by which any of us assimilate information is a complex one. Trying to understand is going to be an important part of coming to terms with mortality. This process will include struggle and pain. There may be anger and a real refusal or reluctance to accept some information. None of us should be forced into acceptance – it will take time to absorb what is going on both in and around us. Sometimes total acceptance never happens – and it is a person's right to fight and resist their destiny. For others, the process of coming to terms with these early stages of adaptation will happen naturally over a period of time.

One of the things to bear in mind is that the dying person's perception of their body may change. The body may be viewed as something alien, separate and negative; it cannot be trusted. At the same time, thoughts and dreams may be disturbing and intrusive. This should be accepted as a normal and natural part of adaptation. It is not easy to maintain a positive and creative sense of one's body image and identity.

Those whom the dying choose to talk to, confide in and trust are a very critical part of the journey. These people, who are likely to be their closest loved ones, should be part of the discussions and planning that make up this early stage of growing into acceptance. It will be important to remember that during this period of uncertainty there will be some considerable anxiety and emotional fragility. This should not be taken as an excuse to over-protect the person but rather as an indication of the extra help or support needed in dealing with this reality. In practical terms this means being willing to talk about disturbing topics and being able to handle vulnerability. There is bound to be distress and there needs to be careful, sensitive and compassionate empathy. The person who is dying needs to have help to see what resources are available and how best to draw on these.

With some acceptance of the situation come a number of questions about the course of the illness, treatment and so on. Some of these can be answered only approximately, if at all. The more possible it is to obtain answers, even if they are only vague, the more possible it becomes to reduce uncertainty. This done, support will need to be given to help all concerned to live with remaining uncertainty.

In this context, the ordering of priorities is an important part of adapting, planning and preparing for the future. A friend or ally or advocate can be a great help in sorting out what needs to be done and in what realistic timescale.

Another thing to bear in mind is that not all of our relationships are perfect. There may be some pain at discovering that one was less close to the inner life of the dying friend or relation than one thought. In relationships there is infinite space for misunderstanding and we may have to accept that there are aspects of our understanding which are shallow and partial. Indeed, we may have to accept that for many years we have been tolerated rather than loved. We may even have to realize that we are less good at this relationship than we believed. These are difficult realities to face.

Most people have little idea about how to respond to a dying person. The situation creates all kinds of barriers. Sometimes it is genuinely difficult to know what to say and perhaps to know what a person needs or wants. These factors conspire to make communication difficult and sometimes impossible, and some friends may simply want to stay away. Much of this can be avoided by an early discussion of what is appropriate behaviour. We need to be guided in part by the dying person as they try to enable others to grasp what is needed. More often than we might realize, the dying person will be glad of the opportunity to talk about their death and about other practical problems. Most dying people prefer empathy to sympathy. That requires of us an effort of imagination, not just kindness. Since this is a period of adaptation for everyone, it is important not to assume that immediate reactions are necessarily an indicator of long-term reactions. Acceptance comes at different rates to different people, and the person who seems least able to cope at the beginning may turn out to be the most able later. Perhaps all human beings need the opportunity to think and feel aloud.

4

Living While Dying

Our explorations need grounding in some of the *practical realities* of how we might live with the knowledge that we are dying or face some of the challenges and questions that our reflections may have thrown up. This chapter is intended for those who are facing a terminal diagnosis and those who try to accompany them on this journey. The theme is our shared commitment to live with the tensions of dying and to continue to live as fully as we can, not 'in general' but in the specific circumstances we now face.

Face death and live

To accept and face death and dying is the first step to living. This is difficult – the diagnosis of illness may have been sudden or unexpected. It is sometimes hard to let go of the natural sense of shock and numbness that results from painful news.

This process of acceptance will take time. There may well be part of you that never comes to terms fully with what is happening. There is no right or wrong way of dying and you need to give yourself time and patience to understand what you think and feel.

There is one critical element in this process. Most of us live for the future: looking forward to a holiday; anticipating retirement or a time when the children are settled – we spend a great deal of energy on plans and diaries looking ahead. To face death is to let go of the future. It is to live in the present. There is no easy way of doing this. We have acknowledged in earlier chapters that opening the heart and mind to death offers us a richer way of living now.

What does my life mean?

The discovery of the reality of death may lead us to take stock of our lives. There will be questions, fears and hopes. Illness can take us in new directions and may lead us to question some aspects of the course and substance of our life. Perhaps new realizations or thoughts may emerge as we engage with the uncertainty of the limitations put on the future. This uncertainty invites us to question and search for meaning in our lives, both in the past, present and future.

Understanding your responses

The way that you respond to all this will be uniquely your own. There may be fear, excitement, anger, loss, grief, denial, hope; or any combination of these emotions.

It will be important not to allow others to prescribe to you how to feel and, indeed, to find friends who encourage you to teach *them* how to feel. This is new and possibly exciting territory, which can open up a deeper and richer way of apprehending living.

Allowing time, space and silence

It may be that you don't want to talk about what is happening at all. It will be important for you to choose and control whom you want to share things with and what you want to talk about. In general, open and honest communications are creative and helpful. When we make our feelings known, other people often respond with care and compassion. How you time all this is up to you – you decide how best to handle the conversations.

Telling your family and friends

When you discover that your death is not far away, it is probable that you will want to tell your family and closest friends, but tell them when you feel able to. If you feel that you can't, then you could consider asking a trusted friend to tell them.

People will react in all kinds of ways to your news. Some will be shocked. Others may cry and need your help to come to terms with the truth. Some might refuse to believe it and others may want to offer a whole range of practical help for you. Some will lack any ability to enter into your situation and will need your skill in handling their awkwardness. They may say or do wholly inappropriate things.

Many will not know how to respond. They may have little idea what to say or do because your illness may arouse in them their own set of fears. They may avoid you altogether. Remember that their own apparent abandonment does not mean that they do not love you.

Children also deserve to be told. They are not different from older people in that they cope with what they know.

They, like all of us, cannot cope with what they do not know. Be as honest with them as you can and explain the situation in language that they can understand. Don't over-explain, but do answer any questions that they might have.

Take as much control as you can in your medical care

We have come to respect the medical profession for their expertise, and as part of this we have been taught that as 'patients' we should be respectful recipients of the care they provide. However, you must remember that it is your body and your life. You have a right to have your questions answered when they are fundamental to your emotional and physical well-being.

Take the opportunity to learn about your illness. There are a number of resource points for information in Appendix Two. Ask your nurses, doctors and other care-givers whenever you have a question.

The point of this gathering of information is that the more you understand about your illness, the better you will understand what is happening to you. This will also include knowing about the areas of your illness where there are no clear answers and where you will have to live with the inevitable uncertainty that living with dying brings. You may not be in control of your illness, but you can and should be in control of your care.

Be kind to yourself and tolerant of your limitations

It is inevitable that your illness or treatment will leave you with less energy. There may well be times when you are tired and your ability to think, make decisions or feel will be affected. Your energy levels may well slow you down. You need to listen to your body and respect what it is saying to you. Nurture yourself and get enough rest. Eat balanced meals and set realistic limits to what you can be and do. Shed responsibilities and leave arrangements to others with a clear conscience.

Saying farewell

Knowing that you are going to die offers you a special opportunity to say goodbye to those you love. Think about how you would like to say goodbye. You may like to set time aside to see people individually. If you feel fit enough, then you might like to consider having a gathering for friends and family. There are many ways of saying goodbye. These include writing letters and giving photographs or videotapes as keepsakes. Those who survive you will cherish these gifts for the memories they stand for.

Finding hope

There is often much conversation about timescales, statistics and averages. How long have I got? How will the illness progress? Sometimes it is possible to answer these questions, but the answers do not always give us comfort. Hope means finding some meaning in life, even as death is in view. It is difficult to be prescriptive about how this is achieved. There are some reflective exercises in this book to assist you in this process, on pp. 5–6, 38–40 and 51.

Embrace your faith

It will be important for you to express your faith in ways that are appropriate to you. You may find comfort in reading the Bible or meditating on spiritual texts. Resources for this are offered in Appendix Four. You may want to have the opportunity to participate in the celebration of Holy Communion or to ask your minister or priest for anointing.

Asking for help

Many of us have been brought up to be independent. What you are experiencing should never be done alone. You need to try to reach out to others. You will know whom you feel comfortable turning to when you feel stressed. Give yourself permission to reach out to others for prayers, support and practical assistance.

Whatever you do, don't isolate yourself and withdraw from the people that care for you. Together you can find comfort, dignity and love.

Listening to other voices

Bob

Part of the lesson of living our dying has been the importance of letting go and putting things right. I have discovered how important it is to take the opportunity to have those conversations and to say those things which so often have remained unsaid. I have learned to trust in God's love and draw faith and assurance from my knowledge that the presence of God has enfolded this last stage of my living. Perhaps it seems strange but I have realized how little I have expressed my love and affection to those nearest to me. Don't ever neglect the opportunity to say to those around you that you care for them and are grateful for what they share with you.

Another thought: I have learnt to forgive and let go of past hurts and pains. I have realized the importance of admitting how my own behaviour and attitude have hurt or estranged people around me. The peace and growth that come through forgiveness are profound. Learn to let go and heal your past hurts.

Jean

One of the aspects of my dying that I have had to learn to embrace is the pain of my condition. Pain is a sensation that hurts. It causes discomfort, distress and sometimes agony. It is very difficult to describe or define pain – it is an individual thing and we can cope with it in different ways.

Trusting health-care professionals hasn't been easy for me. It took some time to come to terms with how my doctor told me about my diagnosis. However, I am learning to trust that whatever the cause of my physical or spiritual distress, pain can be relieved. I am learning to describe my pain and embrace some of the side effects of it.

I have discovered which pain-relief methods work best for me. My pain relief allows me to do what is important to me and to those I care about. Learning to embrace my pain has been a key to living while dying.

Helen

The need for information and choice has been critical for me during this stage of my dying. It has been important to find out as much as possible about my disease. The doctor was able to explain some of this but most of it I have discovered from books. Ignorance is not bliss and the more I know, the better I am able to cope with what is happening.

For the most part I have preferred to have the greater part of my treatment at home. It has been necessary to spend some time in hospital but I have been very impressed with the resources and human skill available from the community.

Having as much power as possible over my own situation has been a critical part of finding peace and comfort in my death. Trust has been enabled as the 'systems and professionals' have empowered me to have all the information I need to make intelligent choices about what is right for me.

Practical implications

- Once the initial shock is over, and more positive thinking is beginning, it is probably a good time to start working out what changes will be necessary. This is not to say that anyone should be pressurized into thinking positively – people need to recover from the shock of bad news in their own good time.

- Losses brought about by the change in one's life expectancy need to be faced and considered realistically. Some enjoyable activities may no longer be possible and this needs to be faced and accepted. It may be necessary to plan for other activities and so gradually to accept the limitations that illness places upon us.

- Similarly the gains involved in dying should be acknowledged. Some areas of life may be enhanced –

perceptions and relationships may be changed and a deeper sense of depth and purpose achieved. On the other hand, some responsibilities can be shed with a clear conscience, even if letting go is, in part, done unwillingly.

- The dying person's emotional response may be complex and, for them, discussing this with others may provide considerable reassurance. Simply to be told that it is reasonable to feel anxious or depressed may be a great help. There may be feelings of guilt, especially if there are possible reasons to implicate the person in their own illness (as when a smoker contracts lung cancer). Talking about the issues can help put them into perspective.

- Similarly, reactions to others may be highly variable. If you are dying, and you find that someone is finding your situation difficult to cope with, don't try and avoid the subject with the intention of trying to make them feel better – more often than not, this will perpetuate the whole problem. Far better to bring the subject into the open, and explain why you are reacting the way you are.

- Identify practical difficulties, prepare for them if possible and work out ways around them if you can. If you find yourself tired a lot of the time, for example, identify the things which tire you most and ask yourself whether it is worth continuing to do them. Routine and structure can make activities less tiring and so, if you are tired, get into the habit of setting aside particular times of the day for occupations like seeing people, going out, or sleeping.

- If a member of your family is the dying person, be aware of the temptation to make a fuss and do everything for them. Living is about doing things for ourselves, and being fussed over and cosseted is likely to make the person feel worse. Try to avoid taking over and so removing autonomy. The person who is dying is likely to be struggling to maintain a sense of self and a personal identity. Remember also that people will often feel guilty if others are put to trouble.

- Similarly, don't immediately give up all the things you find enjoyable in order to devote yourself nobly to your loved one's last days. Far from making the dying person feel loved, it is more likely to make them feel a nuisance. Remember that if there are things to enjoy, then your loved one, even when dying, may be able to share that enjoyment through you.

- Above all, don't run away from the dying person. Cards and flowers are nice, but as an addition to personal contact, not as a substitute for it.

- Remember that the news that one is dying doesn't mean that life will never again be enjoyable. Even in this new situation, it is still possible to experience 'a perfect day'.

- A hard point: not everyone is good with dying or suffering people. Some of us are positively bad at it. We need to be sensitive, if we can, to the need to withdraw when we hinder rather than help – painful or humiliating though this may be.

Celebrating our humanity

Sometimes, when we are facing death, it is important that we should celebrate the human capacity for courage and life – the mystery of the human spirit capable of love and facing loss and change.

You may want to find some quiet space within which you can affirm and reinforce these gifts. Remember that you are in the presence of God and that God's love will carry you through your living. Picture what life might be like if you possessed these qualities to a greater degree and pray for God's strength to face whatever the future may hold.

- *Courage*
  Cherish the courage and acknowledge the courage that has enabled you to face this stage of your life.
- *Patience*
  There will be times when you do not feel strong and you will need time to embrace your feelings.
- *Resilience*
  There is nothing that happens to you that you cannot face – you have experienced difficulties in the past and moved on from them and you have the resilience to do so again.
- *Endurance*
  There will be times of loneliness and hardship. Have the faith that you can endure these periods.
- *Perspective*
  Stepping back from your life can be helpful to enable you to see what has happened and what might happen. This distance can help you move ahead.
- *Humour*
  Never lose your capacity to smile – to laugh does not trivialize your pain. Grief is a curious mixture of emotions. Laughter can provide both strength and relief for your suffering.
- *Openness to others*
  Be open to what others can give you and how they

might be able to help you through this part of your journey.

What can I affirm?

These are just some affirmations – give yourself time to find your own within you. Write them down or think about them with others. These affirmations can help you celebrate your humanity and guide your approach to life.

- I am learning.
- I cherish each moment of life.
- I can grow from pain.
- Life is a gift from God.

5

Preparing for and Facing Death Itself

*Accompanying the dying has taught me to appreciate life
in the moment it is lived. What wears us out is bearing the
burden of thought for the past or the future.*

*Life . . . It begins, it continues, you age, you disappear. It's
a rhythm.*

*Death can transform a human being into what he has been
called to become.*

*To practise death is to practise freedom. A person who has
learned how to die has unlearned how to be a slave.*

(Montaigne)

Demolition

*They have blown up the old brick bridge
connecting the coal works with the coke works.
Useful and unimposing,
it was ever a chapel of small waters,
a graceful arch tooth worked with
yellow bricks notched with red bricks,
reflecting there sudden bright winks
from the Browney – an oval asymmetrical image*

which must have delighted, as fisher-children,
these shiftless but solid grey men
who follow so closely the toil of its demolition.

The digger's head drops and grates and swings up,
yellow fangs slavering rubble and purple brick dust;
but the watchers wear the same grave, equivocal
    expression.
They might be grieving
(their fathers built it, or their fathers' fathers)
or they might be meaning

Boys won't be going to the mine no more.
Best do away with what is not needed.
That's Jock Munsey's lad in the cab there, surely.
Good job it's at home, not away on the telly.

(Anne Stevenson)

Creativity is a yearning for immortality. We human beings
know we must die . . . we know that each of us must
develop the courage to confront death. Yet we must also
rebel and struggle against it. Creativity comes from this
struggle – out of it the creative act is born.

Dying is about learning how to give up what we have
embodied. Being alive is being incarnate, in the flesh.
Dying is giving up form, is being embodied and being
disembodied, being bounded and unbounded. What kind
of language will help us better understand our experience?

Lord, in the quietness, reach out and hold me.
Draw me gently into your peace.
And in the living silence of your heart,

Attune my ears to hear the sounds I never listen to.
The harmony that lies in you, the discords in the dying
    that I embrace.
The laughter and tears in other people's lives.
Make me more sensitive to others' needs.
Sometimes I hear the words that others speak,
But fail to grasp their meaning.

Help me to listen to myself, the hopes and fears, the wor-
ries and the possibilities.
    Help me to hear the voices, the fear wrapped in a
joke, the insecurity behind unbending dogmatism.

Help me to listen more, and think before I respond and
then think again.

And Lord, teach me to hear the sincerity in those who see
and say things in a different way. Give me grace not to
condemn or criticize, but to search for common ground
and grasp the things that draw us all together, not con-
centrate on what holds us apart.

Help me to take the richness of another's thought, and
hold it, precious as my own.

Above all, in my living and in my dying, may I hear the
gentle echoes of your love, reflected all around me. Give
me the joy of listening to your voice, the quiet rustle as
your arms enfold me.

My first job in the ministry was in the north-east of England, in Consett, the former steel town in County Durham. Anne Stevenson's poem sums up many of the changes facing post-industrial society. Many communities across the UK continue to face these challenges. Such experiences represent a death of the familiar and the secure. The local men look on as the bridge is destroyed – a bridge that has stood for generations. The men stand by and watch what for them is the death of their local community, their familiar patterns and the basis for their economic security. It is interesting perhaps to wonder about the nature of these men's grief. Are they grieving? In some ways they have a stoic acceptance of fate and of the somewhat inevitable decline of the region. There is a stubborn clinging to a sense of community in their strange satisfaction that the young driver demolishing the site is a local lad. He has not been forced south for employment but is able to stay close to what is familiar. There is a real pathos and irony here as the machine that the young lad drives spews out the debris of dead industry.

This poem, however distant or removed from our own experience, explores the response to change and loss, which are inbuilt into human existence. As soon as we think of these phenomena, our hearts and minds are filled with our own experiences of loss and those of others who are forced to face change. There are countless unnamed men and women deprived of company and love. More and more people have to live with failures in love, destructive relationships, divorce or unresolved conflict between family members. There are many people who are deprived of food, warmth, clothing and employment. Some individuals find life a real struggle, without meaning or purpose, and there are times in all our lives when we have to face the limitations of being human, especially in relation to our health and scope for creative independence.

This restless process of living, changing and grieving takes us to the heart of our human existence. It is clear that part of our grasp of wholeness and happiness depends on how we cope with these experiences. Tension is not always a good thing, but avoidance and denial can be worse for us as coping mechanisms. This may be particularly true in our relationship with God. Perhaps there is no such thing as an easy, placid and comfortable relationship with God. If we think there is, then perhaps we remain asleep or unborn.

In connection with our preparing for the vulnerabilities of human life and our ultimate destiny, it is worth exploring, in quite a basic way, three aspects of our spiritual lives.

The first relates to our belief and faith. Perhaps the subject of death has challenged you to look again at who you are, where you are going, what you believe to be important and how best you might face death for yourself or others. If our beliefs become cut and dried, then we run the risk of separating ourselves from reality. Faith needs to be able to embrace ambiguity, uncertainty and vulnerability. Perhaps we need to ask ourselves how our faith can become life-giving and effective. How does our faith interact with our lived experiences?

The second area is relationships and love. How do we invest in others as a rich source of growing love and community? Are our friendships able to sustain weakness, failure and insecurity? Are we able to share significant things about ourselves – our hopes and fears, our strengths and weaknesses?

The third area is action – to act in a particular way

means to choose one way rather than another. We have the freedom to choose. We have the freedom to accept our limitations and our mortality or avoid them.

Perhaps the refusal to entertain creative conflict and tension makes us a prey to certain destructive forces. To avoid the symptoms of our mortality, tension or conflict is to risk leaving our spiritual life impoverished and under-developed. There is a danger that God remains no more for us than a compliant parent or a big brother who relieves us of being ourselves. Faith can become no more than a bigoted and blinkered adherence to beliefs whose function is to keep us safe, comfortable and respectable. Love can be disguised narcissism. We imagine that it is God and our neighbour that we see in the pool – but all the time it is ourselves. The danger is that love and concern are kept for ourselves and no one else. Preparing for death is, in part, about living our life to the full and allowing this life to enrich, challenge and free us to travel along different roads to places of freedom, depth and purpose. Preparing for death is about becoming more human and more fully ourselves.

The message here is summed up and has its basis in the words of the Funeral Service: 'In the midst of life we are in death'.

Listening to other voices

Patricia

I am a 55-year-old woman dying of cancer and I'm glad to have the opportunity to share with you some of the elements of my story. Above all I want to live as fully as I possibly can by creating each day, as best I can, a better quality of living. Part of this means planning something worthwhile, because to think ahead gives me the opportunity to fashion the best of what is possible out of the time remaining.

I am surrounded by people who care and many who are very well-meaning. But in the end, I must die my own death. Dying is a journey one takes alone with a crowd. I have learnt to accept as a gift what others want to give me – it sometimes makes them feel better, but I am constantly surprised at what I receive from others, often in unexpected ways.

It has been important for me to be alone and to help others see how important it is to be by myself. I have needed this time to face death, consider it and accept the diverse range of reactions to what is happening to me. It is rather like taking time to gaze at a large, colourful, abstract painting. I'm fascinated by the colour and the light – but it also remains, in part, a mystery. I glimpse fragments of the total canvas which is my life, both seen and unseen.

I have also learnt to trust my own perceptions and reasoning. No one can totally understand what I want or need. Some people 'bully' me with advice that they think helpful but in the end I have accepted that I don't want to give someone else authority over my own feeling, thinking and praying.

Above all, after over 30 years in a demanding job, the hardest lesson has been learning to slow down. I may not have a lot of time, but there is always enough time to think, plan, reflect and prepare.

Paul

At the age of 85 I should have been prepared for death, knowing that I was living on borrowed time. There have been all kinds of matters to 'settle up'. There were people I needed to see, matters to put right, so I could die at peace with others and myself. I needed to be practical about who could help me and what kind of help I needed. I needed someone to guide me through this unfamiliar domain and to know what places or organizations could give me the practical information I needed.

What do I mean? I needed to sort out my finances and make arrangements for my funeral. I needed to know what was happening to my body and how the disease would progress in its last stages. When your body is in danger, you need to do what you can to prolong its utility and to seek to repair that wholeness that has been compromised by illness.

In the end, I needed a place and people where I could reflect on all this at my own pace and in my own way. Perhaps I was surprised at my inmost fears and terrors, my hopes and weaknesses. I had thought that at my age I had all this sorted!

At one level I have feared death all of my life, but now I am confronted with it, I no longer fear it. Perhaps if I had feared death in the past as little as I do now, I would have dared more and better things? Where will this remaining part of my life and death take me? Who knows?

Philippa

I'm coming through this journey now and am able most days to celebrate my life. I feel in control and at peace. I have had the opportunity to look back over my living and remember all the wonderful things that have made me happy. I have discovered all kinds of capabilities in myself that I never knew. Of course this has been a tragic experience, but overall I have grown, changed and developed because of it. All kinds of parts of me are dying and in some ways I shall be glad to let go of this frail, diseased body of mine. Relationships and love never die and I believe that the gift that is me will live on in memory and space. There are so many people who have shaped and enriched this final part of my journey. I thank God for them.

Practical considerations

The approach of death is, frequently, likely to be frightening. In such a situation, no amount of help and advice will eliminate all anxieties for all people. In facing death it is worth bearing in mind the following:

- Don't try to avoid the subject of death in the hope that the dying person won't have to think about it. There are so many things relating to death in our society that we all receive constant reminders of our mortal condition and ultimate destiny. It may be better to confront the issue of death on one's own terms than to try to avoid it and find the worries breaking through when one is least able to deal with them.
- Remember that fears relating to death can take many forms. The fear of death itself may be less worrying than the fear of loss, separation and fear of the unknown. If the dying person can share these feelings with others, it will enable the process of reconciliation and healing to take place.
- We all have a great deal to learn from dying people. They often are very good at dealing with their fear of death and accept their condition calmly. It may be that

others find greater difficulty in accepting dying and death. If you find yourself in this situation, ask yourself why this could be so. If necessary, discuss it with your dying friend. If this acceptance raises fears about death in you, obtain reassurance from an open and honest conversation.

- Don't presume that the dying person doesn't want to talk about the practical aspects of their death, or that to do so is morbid. Many people have a clear idea about where they would like to die, the donation of bodily organs, the relative merits of burial and cremation, and so on. To know that the next of kin are aware of their wishes can go a long way in reducing anxiety associated with dying.

- Be prepared to experience intimations of death in a variety of forms, especially in dreams. Early reactions to such intimations may be disturbing or confusing, but as with conscious thoughts of death, acceptance does occur. When there are advances in one's illness, it's easy to think, 'This is it, the time has come.' However, many diseases have periods of stability interspersed with definite changes. Try to remember that the setbacks are not always permanent and that they often pass. Even a change for the worse, which isn't passing, still doesn't mean that death is imminent. Thinking positively when these setbacks occur will reduce the fears and anxieties.

- Finally, do not give up things that you like doing without a fight. Many people continue with activities that are important to them to within days of their death. A dying person doesn't have to be reduced to a helpless person, perhaps for days or weeks.

Seeing my own death

- How old am I?
- Where am I?
- What time of the day is it?
- What do I see as I look around me?
- What sounds and smells are in the room or place?
- What have I been doing with my life before this time?
- Who is with me?
- What are they saying to me?

What has emerged for you in this exercise?

- What are your feelings?
- What resistances did you feel?
- What insights did you gain concerning your attitudes to yourself, your values, the people you care about – your hopes and fears?
- How can you use your feelings and insights in caring for others who are dying?

6

Resources from the Tradition

Do you not know that all of us who have been baptized into Jesus Christ were baptized into his death? Therefore we have been buried with him by baptism into death, so that, just as Christ was raised from the dead by the glory of the Father, so we too might walk in newness of life.

For if we have been united with him in a death like his, we will certainly be united with him in a resurrection like his.

(Romans 6.3–5)

'Say nothing'

One of the things that strikes the ordinary reader of Mark's Gospel, is the frequency with which the author has Jesus ask that nothing be said about a really rather stupendous happening or insight.

(see Mark 1.44; 5.43; 7.36; and 8.30)

. . . Perhaps if they had kept silent for a while and allowed the experience to mature in them, their words, when they finally did speak, would have had a more lasting value.

In our own society there is a huge public interest in instant response . . . Our society is not one which encourages people to be still, to say nothing, to foster the space and privacy for reflection, and not to speak until ready to do so.

. . . Repression is a bad thing . . . but the opposite of repression is not the dissipation of significant experiences in easy chatter, but rather subjecting them to reflective scrutiny and thus allowing them to find their place in inactive consciousness.

. . . When was there last a sermon encouraging the consolidation of spiritual experience or insight by not talking too much too soon – a sermon on the text 'Say nothing to anyone'?

(Grace M. Jantzen)

It is the purpose of this chapter to place the befriending of death within the context of our faith. For Christians, the pattern of living and dying, of death and resurrection – in our lives – is given meaning by the life, death and resurrection of Jesus Christ. The final meal of Jesus, then the whole Passion, is the central story, which enables us to make sense of our lives. We tell and retell the story, attending to the dereliction of Gethsemane and Calvary, when all that humanly mattered for Jesus – his friends, disciples and followers, his cause, his preaching – simply collapsed and died. The death on the cross was the death of everything for Jesus: he was truly 'forsaken'. We tell and retell the story of his resurrection, ascension and the descent of the Holy Spirit at Pentecost with the realization that we can find new life in Christ. In what happened to him we see hope and meaning and truth for ourselves in our living and dying; in the deaths and resurrections of our own lives.

On the back cover of this book there is a powerful representation of the crucifixion of Christ. Made in steel by an artist who by training and profession is also a surgeon, it captures something of the cost of this act. In it we glimpse a grotesque death endured in agony. The artist understands the physical reality of death; the pressure and pain and process of dying. It is a reflection of a God who has come down to the lowest part of our need. This is a complete and total offering of love and life for us. It becomes for us the new sanctuary of God's presence.

The 'crucified God' is paradox. A God at one with us in so total and costly a self-giving, a God who knows the absence of God from the inside, is able to overcome the power of evil and sin and death. In this earthed sense, the Christian faith is incarnational. It is embedded in a life, not in abstract ideas; a life marked by a love made known to us in those hands pinned by nails to rough wood and there outstretched to embrace the world. Only a God who so engages with us all can bring us salvation, the living hope for which our world longs.

This crucifix, now living in St Mary's Church, Temple Balsall, is seen weekly by 160 primary school children. They find it fascinating but also, sometimes, disturbing. 'What is that skeleton doing hanging there?' one six-year-old asked. Or an adult passing by on a ramble through Warwickshire wondered aloud with me, 'Strange, you Christians, so interested in images of torture.' The passerby continued to express his surprise; was there something pathological here, something obsessively anti-life, in such an interest in sacrifice? Why should any group of people want to celebrate something so far from the centre of normal human activity? What is it in the sufferings of Jesus, which compels such responses in others?

The crucifixion hanging in St Mary's and represented on the back cover of this book was sculpted by Nigel Dwyer, an artist and surgeon. He has reflected on the ways in which the crucifixion has been depicted, and then attempted to reconstruct, with imagination, its meaning.

One common depiction is of Christ perfectly formed, even on the cross. But this seems to deny the sacrifice of his life and the suffering he endured as a result of one of the most dreadful forms of torture and execution devised by humankind. Our artist is unhappy with such denial.

Here are Nigel's reflections:

I would expect that people might have difficulty understanding my reason for producing an apparent skeletal form fashioned from black steel. I did this because it allowed me to suggest the extreme forms of stress applied to both flesh and bone and the stretching and tearing of muscles and tendons and ligaments. The attenuated upper limbs and exaggerated deformed hands were also an attempt to stimulate the imagination of the physical suffering. While I hoped to be able to convey the gentleness and serenity as well as the suffering in the highly abstracted face, I did not want the piece to be beautiful in the traditional sense of elegance, and this was the reason for the use of steel, with all its structural connotations.

This material also allowed me to use welding, not only as a fixative, but also as a decorative medium in its own right, resulting in the piece having an almost gothic or medieval mien. This was not planned but it is, I believe, serendipitous in terms of its ability to live in harmony with the antique beauty of St Mary's. I also designed the sculpture to hang well above the line of vision so that it demands that the observer has to look up at it. My intention here is to allude to the veneration we owe to our Saviour.

The cross is made from reclaimed pine. The chap who sold it to me claimed that it had been taken from one of the inner-city churches that had recently been demolished. Having cleaned the timber, I darkened it with flame until the whole surface was quite black. I then wire brushed this surface until it was slightly burnished and the grain raised.

The result is a powerful and disturbing reflection on the meaning and power of the crucifixion for 'seeing salvation'.

Any church building has the potential to reflect the meaning of God and faith. Every church is a place of gathering, where offering is made, both of all that the people reflect of themselves towards God, and of the glory and beauty of God refracted into the universe.

The cost of this meeting, this gathering, was made possible by the death and resurrection of Christ. There is something deeply compelling in this death. It has led millions of people to shape their lives around the way of the cross. We are Christians because this one man died.

What confronts us in the death of Jesus is actually not something which has been explored in the chapters of this book. But it is something which is not very far from the centre of normal human activity. What we glimpse in the death of Jesus is the pain, hatred and betrayal, the fear and the suffering, which are part of our lives and our world.

In the cross we see ourselves reflected. This one man's

death is a mystery. By mystery we mean here that it represents a truth so deep that all our understanding will be insufficient to comprehend the whole. It will reward prolonged and repeated attention; after we have made our attempts at grasping, there will be much that remains unsaid – what St Paul calls 'the unsearchable riches of Christ' (Ephesians 3.8, AV). This death is a mysterious death because in it and through it God offers a transformation of evil.

The world around us is a strange and complex place in which many are engulfed. In our experience we have to face loss, change and our human limitations. All of us will, by choice or at the inevitable end of our destiny, have to face our own dying and death.

It is within these realities, our human condition, that the love of God is offered to us. This is a love shared through death, the painful death on the cross. It is, as we have noted, a harsh and shocking image, but a reality which can give us life and hope.

The core theme of this book is that our wholeness depends on engaging with the reality of death in us and around us. The promise on the cross is that in and through loss, through befriending our death, there lies the possibility of a surrender to and intimacy with God. We need therefore to learn to become less strong, less confident, less well-defended, less identified with our own idea of God. This befriending of change and loss is part of our attentiveness to the meaning of the cross and to the promptings of the Spirit, as well as to the other person, whoever that person may be. This journey is a pilgrimage to a place of openness, honesty, humanity and vulnerability.

Woody Allen once said, 'I'm not afraid to die, I just

don't want to be there when it happens.' For those who befriend death there is recognition of the importance of staying with our death and loss. It affirms the necessity to discover a capacity to live our lives in all their pain and complexity. This learning to die is the key to our freedom. When we learn this freedom to live our own lives, then death can find its proper place without any morbidity or despair.

The example of someone who has faced loss and death gives us a reflection of a life which displays both self-love and self-gift. The example comes from the diary of Etty Hillesum, a Dutch Jewess who was in her mid-twenties as the Nazi occupiers' drive against the Jews in Holland went into top gear. She was seized by fear, resentments and fatalism. She wrote:

> I want to try to be true to that in me which seeks to fulfil its promise. I have matured enough to assume my own destiny, to cease living an accidental life.
>
> It is no longer a romantic dream, or thirst for adventure, or for love, all of which can drive you to commit mad and irresponsible acts. No, it is a terrible inner seriousness, difficult and at the same time inevitable.

What compels our passionate response is that the death of Jesus is the death of a man who mirrors the mystery and power of God. In this death we see the passion of God, the suffering of God. This suffering shows us more than any other sign the love God has for us. This love is so great that he will live with us and die with us and suffer the pain of all our evil doings.

For to love truly is to suffer. To love another is to risk the pain of losing them, to be hurt when they are hurt; to love is to accept in them not only that which delights us, but to take on also that which does not.

It is a popular lie that there can be love without pain and love without sacrifice, that the word 'passion' signifies the pursuit of pleasure only. Such passion is fantasy and will, in the end, die. True love is love which suffers – and this we find in the love of God which is the passion of Christ.

There is one further theme which the death of Christ opens up for us: forgiveness. We do not know the harm that we do to ourselves and others. Sometimes we never know because our motives, which seemed honest beforehand, turn out on reflection to be corrupt. 'The heart,' says Jeremiah, 'is deceitful above all things.' We know from our own insight of learning that some of the roots of our emotions and actions lie deeply embedded in the recesses of our minds, hidden from us.

Part of what we learn from the death of Christ and its meaning in the Christian tradition is the central reality of sin and the necessity for us to learn to forgive others. The death of Christ asks us to consider the ways in which we hurt each other. When we do something wrong it is easy to think of mitigating circumstances, yet how difficult it is to excuse in others the smallest wrong. We are not content until we have blamed them and got our own back by expressing our anger, healing our hurt by vindictive gossip. Yet sin is a deep and mysterious thing. Each of us has a life history which has left its scars. We have survived the battles of childhood, the fears of dark rooms, the misery of conflict with our families and our playground friends. We have all known the failure of parents that rocks the security that we have expected or hoped to rely on at home. We all experience the guilt and loneliness of growing up. Most face the stresses of work, the worry of parenthood, the loss of much-loved parents; and we have to face the inevitable anxieties of old age.

All these things are part of a normal human life, even when unaffected by disasters, such as war or famine. These things we live with and share sometimes in the hope of understanding and healing; but these hurts lie deep within, fuelling our anger, our fear, our hatred and our scorn, all of which divide us from God and one another.

Jesus placed forgiveness at the centre of his life and death. He understood that each of us must accept our responsibility for the harm that we do. To admit our guilt is an inevitable part of the hard road to freedom. The outcome is forgiveness. The cross is a symbol of the desire of God to save our disordered race from sin. Jesus came to save our disordered race, by himself calling a halt to anger, revenge and cruelty. In the final moments of terror, as the nails are driven through ankles and wrists, there is forgiveness. This is forgiveness, while bestial humankind, with all the scars of all the ages, is absorbed into the love of God. In this embrace there is healing, forgiveness and transformation.

The Gospel writers express their message out of Easter faith. Even the abandonment of the Passion narratives is held within that context. In Mark's Gospel when he speaks to us of the resurrection he does so in a few words – of women going to the tomb on Easter Day, and being overwhelmed by something new and utterly unexpected. The tomb was empty, Christ was risen and they fled in terror (Mark 16.1–8). The women stumbled over an event, which has blown the whole course of human history open and which impels the Church to preach Christ crucified and raised from the dead.

The death of Christ, and our following, embracing and befriending this death is a beginning and not an ending. Jesus has won the victory, and before him and us stretches an endless vista of life and activity. His work continues through us. The tender reception of souls in baptism; the constant giving and loving in the Eucharist; the moulding of many saints into the pattern of perfection; the constant extension through our prayers, our care and our handling of our human experiences of life and loving. In all we do for love, God is active and among us.

The Easter message calls us into this new creation, setting us free to live in the faith that nothing can separate us from the love of God, triumphant over death and every power of evil.

7

Preparing for Your Funeral

O gaping earth!
Receive the body formed of you by the hand of God
and again returning to you as its mother
for what has been made to his image,
the Creator has already reclaimed.
Receive then this your own.

(*Orthodox Liturgy*)

In sure and certain hope of the
resurrection to eternal life
through our Lord Jesus Christ,
we commend to Almighty God
our sister/brother
and we commit her/his body
to the ground/to be cremated
earth to earth, ashes to ashes, dust to dust.

The Lord bless her/him and keep her/him
the Lord make His face to shine upon her/him,
and be gracious,
the Lord lift up His countenance upon her/him
and grant His peace.

(*Common Worship* (adapted))

Earth must go back to earth; then life like all like crops is
harvested.

(Euripides)

On Death

You would know the secret of death.
But how shall you find it unless you seek it in the
heart of life?

The owl whose night-bound eyes are blind into the
day cannot unveil the mystery of light.

If you would indeed behold the spirit of death, open
your heart wide into the body of life.
For life and death are one, even as the river and the
sea are one.

In the depth of your hopes and desires lies your silent
knowledge of the beyond;
And like seeds dreaming beneath the snow, your heart
dreams of spring.
Trust the dreams, for in them is hidden the gate to
eternity.

(Kahlil Gibran)

We have all experienced other people's funerals and this
will, in part, have shaped our sense of what is a good
funeral.

It is the purpose of this chapter to offer some thoughts
about the shape and choices of the funeral service. Death
sometimes occurs suddenly and many people are not given
enough time to prepare for the service. You may want to

play a part in deciding how your life is commemorated. You may want to shape the meaning and significance of the service. It can be of enormous help to the bereaved if they know what your wishes are. By planning your service, you will have led them and helped them towards an appropriate memorial and farewell.

It is important to emphasize the freedom that people have in choosing the sort of funeral they want. The quality of provision is patchy across the UK, but most clergy and ministers are willing to sit down and consider how best the service can honour the dead and express some of the thoughts and feelings which call for expression publicly on such an occasion.

The main elements of a funeral are described below. The ritual and the address are an important part of the provision of a framework within which the mourners can plan the service, make sense of what is happening and take the opportunity to evoke the uniqueness of the one who has died.

Put another way, there are three aspects to the funeral service. The first is to give thanks for the individual and express all that they meant to us. The second is to commend the soul of the deceased into the hands of our Creator (sometimes this may present difficulties to the unbeliever, the agnostic or atheist). The third task is to pray for one another as we grasp the enormity of death.

You should consider: What message do you want to bring to those present at your funeral? What feelings do you want the funeral to express?

Traditionally the messages expressed in a Christian funeral are:

- Faith, hope, love
- Consolation
- Penitence
- Reconciliation
- Celebration and thanks
- Continuing presence
- Eternal life

The funeral service

The basic shape of the religious funeral service is common to many different churches. A typical funeral consists of the following elements:

- The bidding (prayers)
- The Word (the Bible, other readings, the address(es))
- Other readings
- The address(es)
- Prayer (general prayers)
- The commendation and farewell (prayers)
- The committal (prayers)

The bidding consists of the gathering being made welcome by the officiant and their being invited to remember the personality of the deceased, to give thanks and to comfort those who grieve.

The Word is expressed in prayer, in readings, in psalms and hymns and in the address in which the life, work and personality of the deceased finds expression, often in relation to Christian belief in the mercy of God and eternal life.

Prayer will be expressed in the form of prayers and sometimes readings. These will invite the bereaved to remember the deceased and to express their feelings, including penitence for what might have been their own shortcomings in their relationship with the deceased. Prayer can be an opportunity to search the heart and resolve to live a better life. Some funeral services celebrate the Eucharist, for faith celebrates the death and resurrection of our Lord and, at the heart of this celebration, there is the expression of grief, remembrance, thanksgiving and triumph over death. Christian prayer is then both an act of intercession and an expression of solidarity in Christ across the frontier of death.

The commendation and farewell At this point in the service the soul of the deceased is commended to God in the faith that God will grant rest, peace and everlasting life. This is the opportunity for the bereaved, in the presence of the deceased, to say their last goodbyes.

The committal This is the part of the service during which the body in the coffin is lowered into the earth for burial or, at the crematorium, passes into the crematory for disposal.

Some decisions to be made about your funeral

1 Do you wish to be buried or cremated?
2 Where would you like to be buried? Or where might you be eligible to be buried? What should happen to your ashes?
3 What kind of funeral service do you want? (A funeral-only rite, or a requiem Eucharist?)
4 What hymns would you like to have?
5 Have you any particular choice of readings? There will be a biblical reading included in this service but you may want to suggest your own. Your choice of

readings may include a favourite poem or a piece of literature.

6 Would you like any special music to be played or sung, before, after and/or during the service?

7 Would you like a friend/colleague or anyone else to take part in the service? For example: reading a lesson, leading prayers or offering a short appreciation.

8 Would you like to nominate the people to bear the coffin?

9 Have you any other special instructions for the clergy, funeral director or your next of kin?

10 Have you thought about writing anything else down that would help those responsible for preparing the service (the aspects of your life that you would like to celebrate; your own concerns and interests; your journey of faith)?

Practical considerations for those standing by

What should I do when someone I know has died?

When a friend or acquaintance dies you may want help. It is sometimes difficult to know what to say or do. The information here is written as a framework to help you think about how best you might respond to comfort those immediately bereaved.

While you may feel hesitant about intruding on the family during their grief, it is important to visit them. This presence can be an expression of your love and support. Your visit can serve to express to the bereaved that they are not alone and that, while suffering a great deal, they are still connected with the living and that life will go on.

When should I visit?

Upon learning of a death, intimate friends of the family should visit the home to offer sympathy and to ask if they can help.

How long should I stay at a visit?

It is necessary to stay for only a short time. Fifteen minutes or so gives you enough time to express your sympathy. Long, well-meant visits can easily be a trial for all concerned.

What should I say?

Using your own words, express your sympathy. Kind words about the person who has died are always appropriate. If the family wants to talk much at all, they usually simply need to express their feelings and reflections. They are not necessarily looking for a response from you. The kindest response (if it is appropriate for you) might be a warm hug and the expression of understanding. Your simple presence will often mean a lot to the family.

Other expressions of sympathy

It may not always be possible to visit, but there are many other ways to express your sympathy.

Letters
A letter or card expressing what the dead person meant to you is often kept and treasured.

E-mail
E-mail is appropriate, perhaps from those who are not especially close or intimate with the family, such as a business colleague or a former neighbour. The family will appreciate your message of concern.

Flowers
Flowers, usually sent via the undertaker, can be a great comfort to the family. Some people prefer to send flowers to the home afterwards. Remember that sometimes the family asks that donations to a charity should be made in lieu of flowers. Decide whether to send flowers to the house or for the funeral.

Food for the family
One of the most welcome gifts at this time is food. There may be several visitors in the house who need to be fed. Be practical – dishes that require little preparation other than reheating are appropriate.

Mass cards
If the deceased was a Catholic, some people will send a mass card. Some Christians may arrange for a mass to be said for the deceased. Families may feel comforted by the assurance of prayers.

Memorial gifts
Some families appreciate a gift in lieu of flowers. Often the family will designate a specific organization or charity.

Phone calls
Do ring as soon as you are able to offer your sympathy. Try to keep the call brief.

Afterwards

What do I say when I see the family in public?

What you say depends on whether you have already had contact with them. If you have attended the funeral, then take the opportunity to greet them and ask how they are doing. If this is your first meeting with them since the death, you might like to take this opportunity to express your sympathy. It is sometimes difficult for the bereaved to deal with sensitive emotions in a public place. It might be better to find an alternative way of expressing your concern and offering some practical help.

What can I do to help later?

The days and months after the funeral can often be very difficult for the bereaved. We expect people who have experienced death to move on and get back to normal. But they will continue to need help and support. Try to keep in touch. Try to write or call on a regular basis. Continue to include them in your social plans. Try to remember the family on special occasions during the first year following the death. Don't worry about bringing up the pain and emotion of the loss; they are well aware of that. It is important to try to find opportunities not only to remember the death, but also reaffirm that a life was lived.

8

Conclusions

We all have a lust to live. We are born to want: we are born with the feeling of living, and the wish to enjoy life and love our living. The stream of living is akin to the current of a river. It has its own energy and movement and sometimes we have little control over it.

Christ created his own death. He gave himself to it. In his sacrifice our human world of created values and relationships is challenged. So we can learn that dying strengthens our living. The knowledge of dying is an expression of living, of healthy-mindedness, as we become more integrated in ourselves. The theme of this book is that we should befriend death, and open the door of living by engaging with the unknown. Our embracing of dying gives our living a sensitivity, an immediacy, a seriousness and an innocence. This can open up new dimensions about what we hope for and whom we want to become.

Inherent in this living are movement and change. Befriending death is, in part, the story of the movement of our life. A friend asked Plato, on his deathbed, if he would summarize his great life's work in one sentence. Plato looked at his friend and said, 'Practise dying.'

Befriending death finds its goal in our making the dying experience explicit. We are challenged to form connections between images and words and the experiences of dying. We are not victims of dying and it does not victimize us; though we can be victims of shallow, distorted attitudes to dying.

This process of befriending asks us to reflect on what kind of people we are. Most people live their dying as they have lived their lives – as people who rarely express themselves emotionally or spiritually. It is possible to live our lives in denial, misery and defeat and to die the way we live. Are we prepared to be trained to die, to find a rich self-expression, which may nurture our deeper, spiritual selves?

We have noted that there are all kinds of dyings. We are always losing and finding, always breaking with the old and establishing the new. These little dyings may teach us what our death may be like. Befriending our death connects us to our experiences in life in a way which encourages us to self-correction, self-formation and self-expression. Dying and death are not separate events – they shape our humanity and our spirituality.

Dying is about learning how to give up what we have embodied. Being alive is about embracing our humanity, our flesh, our boundedness and our unboundedness. We need to learn to live and die in a way that helps us better to understand both ourselves and all we stand for.

Some reflections and advice from a support group for those facing a terminal illness

- There are lots of organizations set up to help you. Use them.
- Find someone you can complain to endlessly and who will not judge you. Sometimes those who love us best

are too swamped with their own reactions to be able to give us what we need.

- Relaxation techniques are helpful in maximizing your energy and feelings of well-being.
- Try alternative medicine if you think that will help.
- Accept offers of help: lifts, ironing, cooked dishes, treats. People want to do something and if you can bear to receive, it feels good for both givers and receivers.
- Let your GP know if you feel unable to cope or get very depressed.
- Accept that it is OK to refuse to talk about things when you don't want to.
- Don't expect too much of yourself in terms of stamina or energy.
- Look for little things that cheer you up, small comforts to get you through the hour or the day.
- Take someone with you to the doctor or lawyer. Writing down questions before you go in can be useful and it is also helpful to write down the answers.
- Insist that language is used that you understand, and ask for clarification if you are unsure.
- Don't expect to be able to pray, unless you want. Let others pray on your behalf. Feel free to protect yourself from people in situations that are too difficult. Some people are always hard to handle, and you don't need them now.

Appendix One
What to Do After a Death

How to register the death

In normal circumstances the GP will have examined the body recently and will be able to write out a Cause of Death Certificate. This should be taken in person to the registrar appointed for your area (your undertaker, Citizens' Advice Bureau or post office can inform you who your local registrar is) for the death to be registered. Sometimes you might have to ring first to arrange an appointment. The telephone number will be listed under Registrar of Births, Deaths and Marriages. In exceptional circumstances – maybe if you are disabled – the registrar will come to your home to register the death.

However, although the next of kin may feel responsible for doing it, any relative can register the details who:

- was present at the death, or
- was present during the last illness, or
- is resident in the area where the death occurred.

Certain other people who can give direct evidence of the death are also eligible to register the death. All deaths should be registered within five days in England, Wales and Northern Ireland.

There are two purposes for registration:

1   to confirm the identity of the deceased; and
2   to establish the cause of death.

The body can be released for burial or cremation only when the registrar is satisfied about the person's identity and the cause of death.

In most cases, this will be straightforward. As well as the Cause of Death Certificate, the informant needs to take, wherever possible:

- birth and marriage certificates;
- the deceased's medical card;
- any state benefits books.

The registrar will also want to know:

- the full name of the deceased (and the maiden name if applicable);
- any other names the deceased was known by;
- the occupation of the deceased;
- date and place of birth;
- date and place of death;
- last address;
- name, date of birth and occupation of spouse (or previous spouse); and
- whether deceased was receiving any state benefit.

The registrar will then issue a Certificate for Burial (also known as the Green Form). This must be given to anyone organizing arrangements before the funeral can take place.

If cremation is preferred, your doctor needs to complete a form as well as a second independent doctor. Both doctors must certify a cause of death and that no further examination of the body is necessary. Please note that your first costs are incurred here, but normally a funeral director will include these charges in his bill.

This process is not straightforward and it is not easy to remember everything, especially if you are feeling distressed. Remember that the most important piece of paper is the death certificate. This will be a key document for handling the deceased's affairs. You can be given a number of copies to make your task easier.

It is advisable, if you are likely to be in some distress with all the formalities, to take someone along for support.

Who do I need to tell?

This is not a complete list covering everyone's individual circumstances. You should return the following, with a note of explanation and the date of death with each of the items:

- The deceased's passport to the Passport Office.
- Order books, payable orders or Girocheques to the social security office or other office that authorized the payment. This applies also to a child benefit book that includes payment for a child who has died. Orders should not be cashed after the death of a person. It may be useful to keep a record of pension book numbers or other social security numbers;
- The deceased's driving licence to DVLA, Longview Road, Swansea, SA6 7JL;
- The registration document of a car, for the change of ownership to be recorded, also to DVLA;
- Any season tickets, claiming any refunds;
- Membership cards of clubs and associations, again, claiming any refund due;
- Library books and tickets;
- Any National Insurance papers to the relevant office; and
- Any National Health Service or social services equipment such as wheelchairs or hearing aids.

You should tell:

- The offices of the local electricity, gas or telephone company, the water authority and the council (i.e. council tax);
- The local social services department of the council if the person was getting meals-on-wheels, home help or day centre care, or had equipment issued by the department;
- Any hospital the person was attending;
- The family doctor to cancel any care, if they were not involved in certifying the death;
- The Inland Revenue;
- The Benefits Agency;
- Any employer and/or trade union;

- A child or young person's teacher; employer or college if a parent, brother, sister, grandparent or close friend has died;
- The car insurance company;
- The local council housing department if the person who has died was living in a council house;
- The local council housing benefit/council tax benefit section (if applicable);
- The post office so they can redirect mail if necessary; and
- Solicitor and executors regarding the will.

Appendix Two
Information and Resources

Bereavement care information

Befriending Network
St Barnabas Community Centre, 33A Canal Street, Oxford OX2 6BQ
Tel: 01865 316200
Also Claremont, 24–27 White Lion Street, London N1 9PD
Tel: 0207 689 2443

Compassionate Friends
53 North Street, Bristol BS3 1EN
Helpline: 08451 23 23 04 *Administration/Fax:* 08451 20 37 86
A nationwide organization of bereaved parents offering friendship and understanding to other bereaved parents after the death of a son or daughter from any cause whatsoever. Personal and group support. Quarterly newsletter, postal library and range of leaflets. Support for bereaved siblings and grandparents. Befriending rather than counselling.

Cruse Bereavement Care (National Organization for the Widowed and Their Children)
Cruse House, 126 Sheen Road, Richmond, Surrey TW9 1UR
Administration: 0208 940 4818 *Fax:* 0208 940 7638
Helpline (speaking directly to a counsellor): 0870 167 1677 (9.30 a.m. to 5 p.m. weekdays only)
A national organization for bereaved people offering a service of counselling by trained people, a parent circle (group counselling for the widowed parent with dependent children), advice on practical problems and opportunities for social contact.

National Association of Bereavement Services
20 Norton Folgate, London, E1 6DB
Administration/Fax: 0207 247 0617 *Helpline:* 0207 247 1080
An umbrella organization that can suggest help for those bereaved
by the whole spectrum of deaths – from natural causes to post-
disaster counselling.

The National Association of Victims Support Schemes (NAVSS)
Cranmer House, 39 Brixton Road, London, SW9 6DZ
Tel: 0207 735 9166
Support for families of murder victims – through offering time
to talk about the incident. Also support for relatives of murder
victims. Local support schemes throughout the country.

National Association of Widows
National Office, 48 Queens Road, Coventry CV1 3EH
Tel: 024 7663 4848
Support, friendship, information and advice group for widows.
Branches throughout the country.

SAMM (Support After Murder/Manslaughter)
Cranmer House, 39 Brixton Road, London, SW9 6DZ
Tel: 0207 735 3838
National organization offering emotional support to family and
friends of someone who has been killed.

SOS Shadow of Suicide
53 North Street, Bristol BS3 1EN
Helpline: 08451 23 23 04
A group of compassionate friends, set up to help parents of children
who have taken their own lives and to put them in touch with other
parents.

Cancer care information

CancerBACUP (British Association of Cancer United Patients)
3 Bath Place, Rivington Street, London EC2A 3JR
Freeline: 0808 800 1234 *Administration:* 0207 696 9003
A national cancer information service offering advice and emotional support to cancer patients and their families and friends by tele-

phone or letter. Publications on most types of cancer produced in easy-to-understand language, available free of charge to individuals. A London-based one-to-one and group counselling service is available (*Tel*: 0207 696 9000) and there is a one-to-one counselling service in Glasgow (*Tel*: 0141 223 7676).

Cancer and Leukaemia in Childhood Trust
Abbey Wood Business Park, Filton, Bristol BS34 7JU
Tel: 0117 311 2600
Helps families by funding treatment for children, by providing welfare care for the whole family and by promoting clinical research. Publications available.

Cancer Relief Macmillan Fund
89 Albert Embankment, London SE17 7UQ
Tel: 0207 351 7811 *Fax*: 0207 376 8098

The National Cancer Alliance
PO Box 579, Oxford OX4 1LB
Tel: 01865 793566 *Fax*: 01865 251050
The NCA is an alliance of patients and health professionals who are working towards improving the treatment and care of all cancer patients countrywide. To this end they speak at conferences and work with the media, professional bodies, trusts and decision-makers locally and nationally. They have established a track record of patient centres' research, and they provide information on cancer services including a directory of cancer specialists.

Funeral/Memorial services

Crematorium Society of Great Britain
2nd Floor, Brecon House, 16/16a Albion Place, Maidstone, Kent ME14 5DZ
Tel: 01622 688292
Can tell you the nearest crematorium to you. Publishes free booklet, *What You Should Know About Cremation*, and a directory of crematoria.

The Federation of British Cremation Authorities

41 Salisbury Road, Carshalton, Surrey, SM5 3HA
Tel: 0208 669 4521
The only authority that sets codes of practice, monitors standards of operation and offers technical advice. Produces statistical information. Promotes crematorium technicians' training scheme. Publishes advisory handbooks and leaflets, plus *Resurgence*, a quarterly journal.

The Memorial Advisory Bureau

Southbank House, Black Prince Road, London SE1 7SJ
Tel: 0207 463 2020
To meet the demand for the provision of facilities for commemorations after cremation and a reaction against unreasonable restrictions on memorialization. Runs an advisory service for those planning memorial sites and supports individuals in all matters concerning memorialization.

Memorials by Artists

Snape Priory, Saxmundham, Suffolk IP17 1SA
Tel: 01728 688934

National Association of Funeral Directors

618 Warwick Road, Solihull, West Midlands B91 1AA
Tel: 0845 230 1343 (44) 121 711 1343 if calling from outside the UK
Its main purpose is to enhance the standard of funeral service throughout the UK and to be of service both to its members and to the general public. Has a training programme with a Diploma in Funeral Service. It encourages all its members to adhere to its Code of Conduct. Most funeral directors belong to this association.

Natural Death Centre

6 Blackstock Mews, Blackstock Road, London N4 2BT
Tel: 0871 288 2098   *Fax:* 0207 354 3831
An educational charity aiming to improve the quality of dying and to act as a society for those dying at home. Publications include *Living Will* and booklist (for information pack send six first-class stamps), *The Natural Death Handbook*, *Before and After*, and

Green Burial. Also offers workshops, seminars for nurses, information on funerals without undertakers, burial on private land, nature reserve burial grounds, cardboard coffins, etc. Most of its publications are accessible free on the Internet: <http://www.protree.com/worldtrans/naturaldeath.html>.

Pagan Hospice and Funeral Trust
BM Box 3337, London WC1N 3XX
Produces newsletter, information leaflets and does hospital visiting and support.

Ancillary organizations

British Association for Counselling and Psychotherapy
BACP House, 35–37 Albert Street, Rugby, Warwickshire CV21 2SG
Tel: 0870 443 5252
A membership organization for counsellors and those otherwise involved in counselling which also provides a counselling and psychotherapy information service for the general public. An A5 stamped addressed envelope should accompany requests for information.

British Humanist Association
1 Gower Street, London WC1E 6HD
Tel: 0207 079 3580
Concerned with moral issues from a non-religious viewpoint; provides and advises on non-religious funerals.

British Organ Donor Society (BODY)
Balsham, Cambridge, CB1 6DL
Tel: 01223 893636
A voluntary organization offering emotional and informative support to donor, recipient and waiting families, intensive care units and theatre nurses. It supports various aspects of organ transplantation. It supplies and coordinates information requested by professionals, media, involved family and general public.

The Council for Music in Hospitals
74 Queen's Road, Hersham, Surrey KT12 5LW
Tel: 01932 252809/252811 *Fax:* 01932 252966
Provides live concerts given by carefully selected professional musicians in hospitals, homes and hospices throughout the UK. The hospice concerts may take place in a variety of venues, for example, the day room or chapel. If requested, music is taken to individual bedsides.

Institute of Family Therapy
24–32 Stephenson Way, London NW1 2HX
Tel: 0207 391 9150
Counsels bereaved families and those with someone in their family who is seriously ill. The service is free but donations are welcome to help other families.

National Association of Councils of Voluntary Service
3rd floor, Arundel Court, Arundel Street, Sheffield S1 2NU
Tel: 0114 278 6636
Provides information about local councils for voluntary service, who in turn can supply details of local voluntary organizations.

National Council for Voluntary Organizations (NCVO)
Regent's Wharf, 8 All Saints Street, London N1 9RL
Tel: 0207 713 6161
Supplies information about national voluntary organizations. Has sister bodies in Belfast, Edinburgh, Caerphilly and Welshpool. Aims to promote, support and facilitate voluntary action and community development throughout the UK.

Patients' Association
PO Box 935, Harrow, Middlesex HA1 3YJ
Tel: 0845 608 4455
Aims to advise individual patients and carers on patients' rights, complaints procedures and access to health services or appropriate private self-help groups. Promotes patients' interests nationally to government, professional bodies and the media.

Samaritans
The Upper Mill, Kingston Road, Ewell, Surrey KT17 2AF
Tel: 020 8394 8300 (office)
        08457 90 90 90 (national UK helpline)
        00 353 1850 60 90 90 (national Eire helpline)
Always there at any time of the day or night to offer confidential
emotional support to those in crisis and in danger of taking their
own lives. There are 200 centres in the UK and Eire. Look in the
phone book under 'S' for your local branch or call 020 8394 8300.

Welfare State International, The Celebratory Arts Company
The Ellers, Ulverston, Cumbria LA12 1AA
Tel: 01229 581127
Artistic director John Fox offers consultancies for imaginative
memorial services, lanterns, urns, painted coffins, etc. Publications
include *The Dead Good Funeral Guide*.

Will Information Pack
Help the Aged, 207–221 Pentonville Road, London N1 9UZ
Tel: 0207 278 1114
An excellent free information pack.

Woodland Trust
Autumn Park, Dysart Road, Grantham, Lincolnshire NG31 6LL
Tel: 01476 581111
'Plant a tree' scheme to remember loved ones; also commemorative
groves.

Death on the Internet

Death, dying and grief resources. There are large websites which
will provide links to most other sites of interest.

CancerBACUP
<http://www.cancerbacup.org.uk>
Support for people with cancer and their families and friends.

The Desktop Lawyer
<http://www.desktoplawyer.co uk>
Legal information, wills, living wills. You can download sample
proformas for doing it yourself.

GriefNet
<http://griefnet.org/>
This award-winning website is your international gateway to
resources for life-threatening illness and end-of-life care. Our primary mission is to improve the quality of compassionate care for
people who are dying through public education and global professional collaboration.

Hospice Organizations in the UK and Ireland
<http:// www.hauraki.co.uk/hospice_uk>
An up-to-date list of hospice information pages on the Internet.

Kearl's Guide to the Sociology of Death
<http://www.trinity.edu/~mkearl/death.html/>
Unlike many of the more psychologically oriented pages here in
cyberspace, the orientation here is sociological. It is here assumed
that individuals' fears of death and experiences of dying and grief
are not innate but rather are shaped by social environments. This
site has interesting and objective information on homicide and
suicide. The section dealing with the personal impact of death deals
with the loss of a child, widowhood and grief. The list of links to
other sites is good.

London Association of Bereavement Services
<http://www.bereavement.org>
LABS has a good list of links to resources for the bereaved.
Particularly noteworthy is its list of sites for people of different
cultural backgrounds and religions.

Our Loved Ones
<www.ourlovedones.com>
The first serious attempt of a British company to offer a long-last-
ing and professional virtual memorial facility on the Internet (£8 a
year for a minimum of five years).

Natural Death Centre
<http://www.naturaldeath.org>
A fascinating website which looks at death dispassionately. It is particularly strong on resources for alternative funerals. There is a link which gives access to the complete text of the 1994 edition of the *Natural Death Handbook*. A must.

SIDS (Sudden Infant Death Syndrome) Network
<http://sids-network.org>
In Europe, many more children die of SIDS in a year than all who die of cancer, heart disease, pneumonia, child abuse, AIDS, cystic fibrosis and muscular dystrophy combined. This site offers up-to-date information as well as support for those who have been touched by the tragedy of SIDS. This site not only deals with still-birth and neonatal death, but also issues such as sibling grief. Most of the links are to other sites in the USA.

A Virtual Garden of Remembrance
Monuments in the World Wide Cemetery allow people to share the lives of their loved ones in ways that traditional printed death announcements or stone inscriptions cannot. Photographs, moving images and even sounds can be included with a monument. People can create hypertext links among family members, and in doing so forge a genealogy of Internet users and their families online and in real time.

Webster's Guide to Death and Dying
<www.katsden.com/death>
This website represents a large and comprehensive collection of Internet resources with a holistic perspective – one that would be helpful to anyone seeking a wider vision and understanding of the death process. It is focused on death as 'natural' and expected for all living beings.

Appendix Three
Journaling

Exercise 1

One of the themes that has emerged in *Befriending Death* is the growth that is possible when we take time to reflect on what is happening to us. 'Journaling' is the exercise of looking inwards and reflecting on how our minds and hearts are shaped through our struggles in living, loving and dying. Your journal can give you one place (though there may be many others) to express your hopes and fears, your pains and frustrations, your sense of meaning and direction. Your journal can be a place of watch and contemplation.

Sometimes we need the space to muse and just feel; time to turn over things in our minds and to wonder aloud what our lives are about. We search for understanding and perspective. Each of the eight chapters has posed particular questions for us to consider. It is probable they have also challenged our emotions and feelings because some of the questions there go to the heart of our lives and their meaning.

As part of your spiritual explanation, journaling allows you a place to ask, 'Where is God in my experience?' You can think about where and how God has been at work in your life. As you contemplate and reflect and pray, you might uncover God's presence in your life. Journaling can free us to explore interior places in our hearts; to uncover or rediscover how we make meaning through the fabric of our experiences.

The act of reflecting can give you the opportunity to find out how God is present with you. Writing may focus your thoughts and feelings, so that the Spirit can guide you to new understandings. As these discoveries occur, they are preserved in your journal for future record. They provide a fixed point where you can dig deep and give voice to where your spiritual life is at any given point.

Any experience has the potential for being a religious experience. Try to open yourself to God's voice. This is the discipline of making theological meaning out of our experience. This process will help us transform ordinary events into meetings with God. Like Moses (Exodus 3.5) we will be able to hear God speaking to us from our plain and ordinary experiences.

Be flexible and experiment with these ideas. Formulate your own. Try not to be too formal or structured. Random thoughts jotted down and collected in a folder could be priceless gems in the future as you set out on a commitment to understand more of your life. Decide how you might want to share some of these experiences with others. Perhaps journaling will enable you to behold God and give you insight, courage and meaning.

- Reflect on some of the themes that have emerged for you in this book. Take them and write out how they have resonated with you.
- Imagine your own death. Journal about this eventuality. What are you doing? What are your regrets? What do you feel at peace about? Who would you choose to be present with you when you die? What would you like to say and to celebrate? What are your life achievements? Don't be modest!
- What unresolved feelings have you got about befriending death?
- If you are coming to terms with the death of a loved one, try to find a picture of them. Allow your imagination to run free about your loved one. What is the person saying or doing? Why is the picture important to you? What special memories does the picture hold for you? How is God present for you in your life together?
- What unresolved feelings have you got about your loved one? Write a conversation that never took place but that you wish had done so. What would you have wanted to share with your loved one (expressions of love, forgiveness/reconciliation, unresolved anger . . .)?
- Reflect on how you think God is present in these experiences and reflections. Write about your experiences of God through your own befriending of death, of your loved one, of your own destiny, your vision and feelings. Write about your feelings towards God (peace, companionship, anger, strength), remembering that the love of God embraces all of this.

Journaling

- On your journey through your illness, or your loved one's illness, what words did you find helpful? What words or advice did someone offer that you found offensive or unhelpful? Reflect on these words and why you feel the way you do about them.
- What memories about your life and your loved ones would you want to be preserved for your children? Write about this legacy.
- How might your loved ones keep living through you? Reflect on these traits (good and bad) and how you want to develop these parts of yourself.
- Draw a picture or make a collage of images that express your thoughts and ideas.
- Write the prayers of your heart in your journal and save them for when prayer seems difficult.

Exercise 2

Reflecting on someone who has died

This is a similar exercise to the above reflections. You may find it helpful to 'sort out' your thoughts about your loved one by writing a letter to the person who died.

Try to express your thoughts and feelings about:

- A special memory that I have about you . . .
- What I miss most about you and our relationship . . .
- What I wish I had said or had not said . . .
- What I'd like to ask you . . .
- What I wish we'd done or had not done . . .
- What I have had the hardest time dealing with . . .
- Ways in which you will continue to live on in me . . .
- Special ways I have for keeping my memories of you alive . . .

Choose one or several ideas that are important to you or start at the top of the list and work your way down. These topics may help you come up with ideas specific to your situation and relationship.

Appendix Four

Prayers and Spiritual Readings

Every death is unique and it is not possible nor desirable to make a single provision to suit all occasions.

I have made a selection of texts from which some choice can be made. Allow time and space for reflection. They may be used, too, by the living, who want to reflect on befriending death.

On Considering Death

Lord, make me an instrument of thy peace.
Where there is hatred, let me sow love;
where there is injury, pardon;
where there is doubt, faith;
where there is despair, hope;
where there is darkness, light;
where there is sadness, joy.

O Divine Master, grant that I may not so much seek
to be consoled as to console;
to be understood as to understand;
to be loved as to love.

For it is in giving that we receive;
it is in pardoning that we are pardoned;
and it is in dying that we are born to eternal life.

(St Francis of Assisi)

Give ear, O Eternal God, to my prayer,
heed my plea for mercy.

In my time of trouble I call you,
for you will answer me.

When pain and fatigue are my companions,
Let there be room in my heart for strength.

When days and nights are filled with darkness,
Let the light of courage find its place.

Help me to endure the suffering and dissolve the fear,
Renew within me the calm spirit of trust and peace.

(Gate of Healing)

Serenity Prayer

God grant me the serenity,
To accept the things I cannot change,
The courage to change the things I can,
And the wisdom to know the difference.

Living one day at a time;
Enjoying one moment at a time;
Accepting hardship as a pathway to peace;
Taking, as you did, this sinful world as it is,
not as I would have it;
Trusting that you will make all things right
if I surrender to your will;
That I may be reasonably happy in this life,
And supremely happy with you for ever in the next.

(Reinhold Niebuhr)

My Lord God

I have no idea where I am going. I do not see the road ahead of me.
I cannot know for certain where it will end. Nor do I really know
myself, and the fact that I think that I am following your will does
not mean that I am actually doing so. But I believe that the desire
to please you does in fact please you. And I hope I have that desire
in all that I am doing. I hope that I will never do anything apart
from that desire. And I know that if I do this you will lead me by
the right road though I may know nothing about it.

Therefore will I trust you always though I may seem to be lost and in the shadow of death. I will not fear, for you are ever with me, and you will never leave me to face my perils alone.

(Thomas Merton)

Lord, when we are weak
we pray without urging (if not without ceasing).
When she is stricken with cancer
or our foundations crumble
when we are scared
shattered
sad
or things disintegrate
we cry out for Your help.
For that we are not ashamed;
we have no regret.

But when we are strong
when it's summertime and life is easy
when all's right with our world and You're safely in heaven
when we have that sense of well-being
Lord, do not let us be
but turn our seeming strength into gratitude
our well-being into thanksgiving
and our recreation into re-creation.
In winter and in summer
no less when pride seduces than when despair overwhelms
when we collapse
and when all heaven breaks loose
when we are weak
and when we are not
Lord, leave us not
to our own defenses. Amen

(Frederick Ohler)

O God, early in the morning I cry to you.
Help me to pray
And to concentrate my thoughts on you;
I cannot do this alone.
In me there is darkness,

But with you there is light;
I am lonely, but you do not leave me;
I am feeble in heart, but with you there is help;
I am restless, but with you there is peace.
In me there is bitterness, but with you patience;
I do not understand your ways, but you know the way
    for me . . .

Restore me to liberty,
And enable me so to live now
that I may answer before you and before humanity.
Lord, whatever this day may bring,
Your name be praised.

(Dietrich Bonhoeffer)

We are often tempted to 'explain' suffering in terms of 'the will of God'. Not only can this evoke anger and frustration, but also it is false. 'God's will' is not a label that can be put on unhappy situations. God wants to bring joy not pain, peace not war, healing not suffering.

Therefore, instead of declaring anything and everything to be the will of God, we must be willing to ask ourselves where in the midst of our pains and sufferings we can discern the loving presence of God.

(Henri Nouwen)

From Scripture

I saw a new heaven and a new earth; for the first heaven and the first earth had passed away, and the sea was no more. And I saw the holy city, the new Jerusalem, coming down out of heaven from God, prepared as a bride adorned for her husband. And I heard a loud voice from the throne saying, 'See, the home of God is among mortals. He will dwell with them; and they will be his peoples, and God himself will be with them; he will wipe every tear from their eyes. Death will be no more; mourning and crying and pain will be no more, for the first things have passed away.' And the one who was seated on the throne said, 'See, I am making all things new . . .' Then he said to me, 'It is done! I am the Alpha and the Omega, beginning and the end. To the thirsty I will give water as a gift from the spring of the water of life.'

(Revelation 21.1–6)

For since we believe that Jesus died and rose again, even so, through Jesus, God will bring with him those who have died . . . so we will be with the Lord for ever. Therefore encourage one another with these words.

(1 Thessalonians 4.14, 17–18)

I am convinced that neither death, nor life, nor angels, nor rulers, nor things present, nor things to come, nor powers, nor height, nor depth, nor anything else in all creation, will be able to separate us from the love of God in Christ Jesus our Lord.

(Romans 8.38–9)

Prayer of Commendation

Go forth upon your journey from this world, O Christian soul, in the name of God the Father almighty who created you; in the name of Jesus Christ, who suffered death for you; in the name of the Holy Spirit, who strengthens you; in communion with Mary and all the blessed saints and aided by the angels and archangels, and all the armies of the heavenly host. May your portion be this day in peace and your dwelling the heavenly Jerusalem.

N, our companion in faith, the Lord who gave you to us is taking you to himself. He who died for you and rose again from death, is calling you to enjoy the peace of the heavenly city in which there is neither sorrow nor pain, and where weakness is transformed into strength. He is calling you to see him face to face that you may be made like him forever. He comes to welcome you with angels and archangels and all his faithful people that you may know in its fullness the fellowship of the Holy Spirit. Enter into the joy of your Lord and give glory to him, Father, Son and Holy Spirit.

Into your hands, Lord, our faithful creator and most loving redeemer, we commend your child N, for he/she is yours in death as in life. In your great mercy, fulfil in him/her the purpose of your love; gather him/her to yourself in gentleness and peace, that, rejoicing in the light and refreshment of your presence, he/she may enjoy that rest which you have prepared for your faithful servants; through Jesus Christ our Lord.

(*Ministry to the Sick*)

At the time of death

N our companion in faith and sister in Christ,
we entrust you to God who created you.
May you return to him who formed you from the dust of
　the earth.
May the angels and the saints come to meet you
as you go forth from this life.
May Christ who was crucified for you
take you into his kingdom.
May Christ, the Good Shepherd,
give you a place within his flock.
May he forgive you your sins
and keep you among his people.
May you see your Redeemer face to face
and delight in the vision of God for ever. Amen

Into your hands, O merciful Saviour, we commend your servant N.
Acknowledge, we humbly beseech you, a sheep of your own fold, a
lamb of your flock, a sinner of your own redeeming. Receive her/him
into the arms of your mercy, into the blessed rest of everlasting peace,
and into the glorious company of the saints in light. Amen

(Common Worship)

Master, now you are dismissing your servant in peace,
according to your word;
for my eyes have seen your salvation,
which you have prepared in the presence of all peoples,
a light for revelation to the Gentiles
and for glory to your people Israel.

(Luke 2.29–32)

We give thanks to you, Lord our God,
for the life of your servant N,
who has passed from this world.
We thank you for . . .
We are glad that we shared some part of her/his life
and now entrust her/him to you.
O God of the living and the dead. Amen

(Common Worship)

Further prayers after death

Father of all,
we pray to you for those we love, but see no longer.
Grant them your peace; let light perpetual shine upon them;
and in your loving wisdom and almighty power, work in
    them the good purpose of your perfect will;
through Jesus Christ our Lord. Amen

(*Common Worship*)

After release from suffering

We thank you, loving Father,
for taking N from sickness into health,
and from suffering into joy.
Grant that those whom he/she has left
may be strengthened by your continuing presence,
and share with him/her your gift of eternal life. Amen
(*Prayers for Use at the Alternative Services*)

After sudden death

O Lord, before you brought us into this world, you knew us.
You knew the number of days this man/woman would live,
but you hid it from us for your own good purposes.

What is sudden to us was known to you before it came to be.
Help us to accept it and to bear it in your strength that
    your name may be glorified and your people sustained;
through Jesus Christ our Lord. Amen
(*A New Zealand Prayer Book*)

O Lord, hear us in our pain and anguish now that N has
    gone from us.
We are bewildered and confused;
let us find rest in you.
Help us to acknowledge and accept what has happened
and to bear it in your strength. Amen
(*A New Zealand Prayer Book*)

101

After a suicide

Lord Jesus Christ,
you knew the agony of the garden and the loneliness of
the cross,
but remained in the love of your Father.
We commend N to your mercy and, claiming no judgement
for ourselves,
commit him/her to you, the righteous judge of all,
now and for ever. Amen

(Pastoral Care of the Sick)

Compassionate God,
we entrust into your care N who has died by his/her own hand.
Grant that the knowledge of your love and mercy may
comfort those who grieve for him/her.
Strengthen our assurance of your redeeming purpose for
all your children,
through Jesus Christ your Son. Amen

(Pastoral Care of the Sick)

Lord Jesus Christ,
you knew the agony of dying alone and abandoned.
We cannot know the agony which led N to take his/her
own life.
We grieve that we could not meet his/her needs.
Console us in the face of death's seeming triumph,
forgive us for failing N in his/her time of need,
and give us the assurance that you can bring hope in our pain.

(Pastoral Care of the Sick)

Comforting the bereaved

We give him/her back to thee, dear Lord, who gavest
him/her to us.
Yet, as thou dost not lose him/her in giving,
so we have not lost him/her by his/her return.
Not as the world giveth, givest thou, O Lover of Souls.
What thou gavest, thou takest not away;

for what is thine, is ours also, if we are thine.
And life is eternal and love is immortal.
And death is only an horizon,
and an horizon is nothing save the limit of our sight.
Lift us up, strong Son of God, that we may see further.
Cleanse our eyes that we may see more clearly.
Draw us closer to thyself, that we may know ourselves nearer
to our beloved who is with thee.
And while thou dost prepare a place for us,
prepare us too for that happy place,
that where he/she is, and thou art, we too may be.
Through Jesus Christ our Lord. Amen
> (Adapted from *The Order of Christian Funerals*)

Prayers for those who mourn

Almighty God, look with pity upon the sorrows of your servants for whom we pray. Remember them, Lord, in mercy; nourish them with patience; comfort them with a sense of your goodness; lift up your countenance upon them; and give them peace; through Jesus Christ our Lord. Amen

> (*Common Worship*)

O God, whose ways are hidden and thy works most wonderful,
who makest nothing in vain and lovest all that thou hast
    made;
comfort thou thy servants, and grant that they may so love
    and serve thee in this life,
that they obtain the fullness of thy promises in the world
    to come;
through Jesus Christ our Lord. Amen

> (*Common Worship*)

Almighty God, Father of mercies and giver of comfort;
deal graciously, we pray, with all who mourn;
that, casting all their care on thee,
they may know the consolation of your love;
through Jesus Christ our Lord. Amen

> (*Common Worship*)

God of all consolation, in your unending love and mercy for us, you turn the darkness of death into the dawn of new life. Show compassion to your people in their sorrow. Be our refuge and our strength to lift us from the darkness of this grief to the peace and light of your presence. Jesus Christ, by dying for us, conquered death and, by rising again, restored life. May we then go forward eagerly to meet him. And after our life on earth, be reunited with our brother/sister where every tear will be wiped away. This we ask through the same Jesus Christ our Lord. Amen

(Common Worship)

O Lord Jesus Christ, God of all consolation, whose heart was moved to tears at the grave of Lazarus, look with compassion on your children in their loss. Strengthen them with the gift of faith, and give to their troubled hearts and to the hearts of all the light of hope, that they may live as one day to be united again, where tears shall be wiped away, in the kingdom of love; for you died and were raised to life with the Father and the Holy Spirit, God, now and for ever. Amen

(Common Worship)

The Communion of Saints

> O what their joy and glory must be,
> Those endless Sabbaths the blessed ones see!
> Crown for the valiant; to weary ones rest;
> God shall be all, and in all ever blest.
>
> Truly Jerusalem name we that shore,
> 'Vision of peace', that brings joy evermore!
> Wish and fulfilment can severed be ne'er,
> Nor the thing prayed for come short of the prayer.
>
> We, where no trouble distraction can bring,
> Safely the anthems of Sion shall sing
> While for thy grace, Lord, their voices of praise
> Thy blessed people shall evermore raise.

Low before him with our praises we fall,
Of whom, and in whom, and through whom are all;
Of whom, the Father, and through whom, the Son;
In whom, the Spirit, with these ever One.

(Peter Abelard, tr. J. M. Neale)

O almighty God, who hast knit together thine elect in one communion and fellowship, in the mystical body of thy Son Christ our
Lord; grant us grace so to follow thy blessed Saints in all virtuous
and godly living, that we may come to those unspeakable joys,
which thou hast prepared for them that unfeignedly love thee;
through Jesus Christ our Lord.

(*Book of Common Prayer*)

Great is the power of thy cross, O Lord! It was set up in the place
of the skull, and it prevails in all the world; it made the fishermen
into apostles and the Gentiles into martyrs, that they might inter-
cede for our souls.

Great is the power of thy martyrs, O Christ! Though they lie in their
tombs, they drive out evil spirits and fight in defence of true devotion,
subduing the dominion of the enemy though faith in the Trinity.

The prophets, the apostles of Christ and the martyrs, have taught
mankind to sing the praises of the consubstantial Trinity; they have
given light to the nations that were gone astray, and they have made
the sons of men the companions of the angels.

(Vespers in Holy Week, *Orthodox Liturgy*)

Spiritual readings

God creates a world which includes among its infinite variety of
wonders this culminating wonder.

In recent theological thinking much has been made of man's role
in sharing or even extending the creativity of God. Man has been
seen, primarily, as 'fellow-worker with God' – as participator, albeit
on a humble scale, in God's everlasting activity of remaking and
redeeming the world. Perhaps this understanding of man's role
needs to be balanced by the perception of man as a 'fellow receiver
of God'. The phrase is unfamiliar and inelegant; and strictly speaking, it would be correct to use instead the more familiar phrase

'fellow sufferer with God'. But the word 'suffer' has come to have, over the years, an ever narrower connotation, and its associations are now restricted to 'pain', 'hardship', 'distress'. It is in a much wider sense than this that man is fellow-sufferer with God. He is one who, like God, is handed over to the world, to wait upon it, to receive its power of meaning: to be the one upon whom the world bears in all its variety and intensity of meaning: to receive upon his transforming consciousness no mere photographic imprint of the world but its wonder and terror, its vastness and delicacy, its beauty and squalor, its good and evil. It is in this dimension – the dimension of meaning – that man receives the world; and as he does so, a figure exposed and waiting, he appears no diminished or degraded figure but a figure of enormous dignity. As he waits on the future, increasingly dependent on systems and machines, on organization and technology, on medical support and social provision, he will in no sense be deprived of his high calling – that of standing beside God and receiving into the transforming mirror of his consciousness what the world really is. Whenever he so stands, in the future as in the past and present, man will be a figure of unique and almost unbelievable dignity.

(W. H. Vanstone)

Our knowledge of God now is the promise and the foretaste of heaven: apart from this present knowledge of God, we should have no clue to what heaven will be; for heaven is God. But it's just as true the other way about – without the heavenly promises God has given us, we should have no understanding of our present life with God. How could we make sense of the journey if we didn't know where the road leads? Unless the promise of heaven was shown to us, how should we guess that the fitful gleams of spiritual light which visit us here, flowed out from the steady and irresistible dawning of eternal day?

Compared with the sight of God in heaven our present glimpses of him seem little or nothing indeed; and yet they are not altogether nothing. Even today, when we pray, the hand of God does somewhat push aside that accursed looking glass, which each of us holds before him, and which shows each of us our own face. Only the Day of Judgement will strike the glass for ever from our hands, and leave us nowhere reflected best by the pupils of the eyes of God. And then we shall be cured of our self-love, and shall love, without even the power of turning from it, the face that is lovely in itself, the face of God; and passing from the great Begetter to what is begotten by him, we shall see his likeness in his creatures, in angels and in blessed saints; returning at long last the love that has been lavished on us, and reflecting back the light with which we have been illuminated. To that blessed consummation, therefore, may he lead all those for whom we pray, he who is love himself, who came to us at Bethlehem, and took us by the hand.

(From 'The Ultimate Hope', a sermon preached in
St Andrew's, Headington, Oxford, a few days before his death in
December 1968, by Austin Farrer)

Love's work

A crisis of illness, bereavement, separation, natural disaster, could be the opportunity to make contact with deeper levels of the terrors of the soul, to loose and to bind, to bind and to loose. A soul, which is not bound, is as mad as one with cemented boundaries. To grow in love-ability is to accept the boundaries of oneself and others, while remaining vulnerable, woundable, around the bounds. Acknowledgement of conditionality is the only unconditionality of human love. (Gillian Rose)

O eternal and most gracious God, who though thou didst permit darknesse to be before light in the Creation, yet in the making of light, didst so multiple that light, as that it enlightened not the day only, but the night too, though thou have suffered some dimnesse, some clouds of sadnesse, and disconsolatenesse to shed themselves upon our soules, we humbly blesse, and thankfully glorifie thy holy name, that thou hast afforded us the light of thy spirit, against which the prince of darknesse cannot prevaile, nor hide his illumination of our darkest nights, of our saddest thoughts. Let thy merciful providence so governe all, that those shadowes which doe fall upon us may be overcome by the power of thine irresistible light, the God of consolation; that thy spirit may disperse them, and establish us in so bright a day here, as may bee a Judgment upon ourselves, and that the words of thy Sonne, spoken to his Apostles, may reflect upon us, Behold I am with you alwaes, even to the end of the world. Amen　　　　　　　　　　　　　(John Donne)

Bibliography

Abelard, Peter, see *Prayers for Use at the Alternative Services*, below.

Ainsworth-Smith, Ian and Peter Speck, *Letting Go* (London, SPCK, 1982).

Anke, Sr., *The Creativity of Diminishment* (Oxford, SLG Press, 1990).

Baisley, B., *No Easy Answers: An Exploration of Suffering* (London, Epworth, 2000).

Beausobre, I., *Creative Suffering* (Oxford, SLG Press, 1984).

Blake, William, 'Auguries of Innocence', *The Oxford Book of Mystical Verse* (Nicholson & Lee, 1917).

Bonhoeffer, Dietrich, in *The Oxford Book of Prayer* (Oxford, OUP, 1985), p. 223.

Boston, Sarah and Rachael Trezise, *Merely Mortal* (London, Methuen, 1987).

Bregman, Lucy, *Beyond Silence and Denial* (Kentucky, Westminster/ John Knox, 1999).

Cassidy, S., *Light from the Dark Valley* (London, DLT, 1994).

Cassidy, S., *Sharing the Darkness* (London, DLT, 1994).

Common Worship: Pastoral Services (London, Church House Publishing, 2000).

Dunn, Michael, *The Good Death Guide* (Oxford, How To Books, 2000).

Enright, D. J. (ed.), *The Oxford Book of Death* (Oxford, OUP, 1983).

Farrer, Austin, 'The Ultimate Hope', in Leslie Houlden (ed.), *The Essential Sermons* (London, SPCK, 1991), p. 203.

Gate of Healing (Central Conference of American Rabbis, 1988), published privately.

Gibran, Kahlil, *The Prophet* (London, Heinemann, 1980), p. 93.

Harvey, Nicholas Peter, *Death's Gift* (London, Epworth Press, 1985).

Hauerwas, S., *Naming the Silences: God, Medicine and the Problem of Suffering* (Edinburgh, T. & T. Clark, 1994).

Hillesum, Etty, *An Interrupted Life* (New York, Mass Market Paperbacks, 1985), p. 212.

Horne, Brian, *Imagining Evil* (London, DLT, 1996).

Hughes, Gerard, *God of Surprises* (London, Darton, Longman & Todd, 1986), pp. 9, 63.

Ironside, Virginia, *'You'll Get Over It'* (London, Penguin Books, 1996).

Israel, Martin, *The Pain that Heals* (London, Hodder & Stoughton, 1981).

Jantzen, Grace M., 'Editorial', *Theology*, 1985, January, February.

Kearney, Michael, *Mortally Wounded* (Dublin, Marino Books, 1996).

Lee, Carol, *Good Grief* (London, Fourth Estate Limited, 1994).

Loyola, Ignatius, *Spiritual Exercises* (Louis Puhl edition, Chicago, Loyola University Press).

Merton, Thomas, *Thoughts in Solitude* (New York, Continuum, 1975), p. 29.

Ministry to the Sick (London, Central Board of Finance of the Church of England, 1983).

A New Zealand Prayer Book (London, Collins, 1986).

Niebuhr, Reinhold, see *Prayers for Use at the Alternative Services*, below.

Nouwen, Henri J. M., *A Letter of Consolation* (Dublin, Gill & Macmillan, 1983).

Nouwen, Henri J. M., *Show Me the Way* (New York, Crossroad Publishing, 1992), p. 45.

Ohler, Frederick, in *Better than Nice and Other Unconventional Prayers* (Louisville, Westminster/John Knox, 1989), p. 112.

The Order of Christian Funerals (London, International Committee on English in the Liturgy, 1989).

Pastoral Care of the Sick (London, Geoffrey Chapman, 1983).

Prayers for Use at the Alternative Services (London, Mowbray, 1986).

Rinpoche, Sogyal, *The Tibetan Book of Living and Dying* (London, Rider, 1992).

Rose, Gillian, *Love's Work* (London, Chatto & Windus, 1995).

Spufford, Margaret, *Celebration* (London, Fount Paperbacks, 1989).

Stevenson, Anne, 'Demolition', *The Fiction Makers* (Oxford, OUP, 1985), p. 38.

Surin, Kenneth, *Theology and the Problem of Evil* (Oxford, Blackwell, 1986).

Bibliography

Taylor, Allegra, *Acquainted with the Night* (London, Fontana Paperbacks, 1989).

Thomas, R. S., 'The Kingdom', *Collected Poems* (London, Dent, 1993), p. 233.

Tournier, Paul, *Creative Suffering* (Geneva, Editions Labor et Fides, 1981).

Vanstone, W. H., *The Stature of Waiting* (London, DLT, 1982).

Walters, Geoff, *Why do Christians Find it Hard to Grieve?* (Carlisle, Paternoster, 1997).

Wilcock, Penelope, *Spiritual Care* (London, SPCK, 1996).